SPIRITUAL CONSTIPATION

Discover Your True Nature
& Get Shift Moving

STEPHEN LADD

APOCRYPHILE
PRESS

To all the frustrated spiritual seekers
and worn-out personal development peepers

May you find Peace
May you know Love
May you be overwhelmed by Grace

"Sooner or later, we all end up
naked on the cross
of our most cherished beliefs." *

* Notes *to self:*

1) pack sunscreen
2) start manscaping

Apocryphile Press
PO Box 255
Hannacroix, NY 12087
www.apocryphilepress.com

Copyright © 2022 by Stephen Ladd
ISBN 978-1-955821-87-2 | paper
ISBN 978-1-955821-88-9 | ePub
Printed in the United States of America

Please join our mailing list at
www.apocryphilepress.com/free
We'll keep you up to date on all our new releases, and we'll also send you a FREE BOOK. Visit us today!

contents

introduction

Do you smell that?

Just to be safe, let's clear the air.

I
don't
know
shit.

Rest assured, this is not my lame attempt to feign humility.

On the contrary, I suppose it may be closer to a false bravado. For let there be no doubt, I forget daily that I'm still quite full of it; and by "it" I mean knowledge. For the better part of four decades, I was a collector, perhaps borderline hoarder, of seemingly pertinent *information*.

And then I mistakenly took information to be *knowledge*; before making the ever-so-popular leap of believing knowledge and *wisdom* were synonymous.

Public Service Announcement: synonyms they are not.

Like many people striving for self-improvement or spiritual evolution, I

adopted an "Acquisition Model Approach," adding all the latest and greatest practices until I just ended up feeling
stuck,
confused,
and constipated.

Every new philosophical model, spiritual path or self-help technique seemed to work, until it didn't.

I felt better,
until I didn't.

I knew this was IT,
until it obviously wasn't.

My assumption was I hadn't found the right teachings (yet) that would shower down upon me the heavenly wisdom I desired more than most anything else in the world. I kept searching, seeking, and filling myself with more. It was discouraging, frustrating, and thoroughly exhausting.

It had never occurred to me that I might need LESS, I may need to do some UN-learning; I was simply short on available bandwidth and would benefit from clearing my mental/emotional/spiritual cache.

So, that is what I did. I literally and figuratively unplugged. I imagined my brain to be an Etch-A-Sketch and gave it an oscillating waggle or three, leaving me with a clean slate, some SPACE. I gave away over 60 self-help and spiritual books. You'll want to do the same with this book immediately upon finishing—or maybe even now, if you've already had enough.

That created space on my mental bookshelf for the first time in decades.

Space...

(like this, sorta)

THAT was the crucial element all along. There just needed to be enough room for insights and innate wisdom to come forth and overwhelm me.

Here's to your own wisdom and the beauty of being overwhelmed by it.

The Foundational
Orientation of this Book

The perspective from which this book is written, and the one I invite you to ponder within while reading, is an amalgamation of my personal four decades (and counting) of self-exploration.

Let there be no doubt: it is a hodgepodge of innate wisdom (primarily borrowed from others far wiser than myself), as well as my own intuition and embodied experiences.

Hodge·podge {HP}

/'häj päj/
a confused mixture, a jumble

My current hodgepodge was determined by whether a perspective/belief/practice would sit nicely within the common area of the Venn Diagram below (there are two types of people in this world, those who love Venn Diagrams, and those who are wrong; see second VD for visual reference):

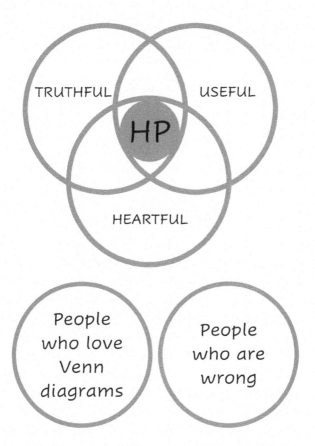

I came to find that basing my understanding of myself and the world—and subsequently any actions—on a perspective that didn't encompass all three principles of being *Truthful, Useful and Heartful* always led me astray in one way or another.

Note: I regard "useful" to also mean "do-able" within "Relative Reality" (we'll chat more about this later). As an example, *ahimsa* is a word from the Hindu, Buddhist, and Jainist traditions meaning to hold a deep respect for all living things and taking a vow to avoid violence towards others.

I focused much of my graduate studies on the Jains, as they were the most extreme in their position on non-violence—the CrossFit of Indian religious philosophies, if you will. This included brushing the area in front of your feet as you walked, so as not to inadvertently step on and do violence to small insects. Obviously, travel by car or plane would unleash a subtle yet substantial pancrustacean hexapod invertebrate bloodbath.

So, instead of throwing the ahimsa baby out with the bathwater, as that would be a bit too overtly violent, I regularly amend and massage these positions to what is possible and feels in alignment with my heart.

Whenever in doubt, I default to what is Heartful.

If you choose to utilize my Hodgepodge VD, I suggest you amend and massage your way through it as well.

Descriptive vs. Prescriptive & Application vs. Implication

Just a heads-up: I will not be telling you how to live your life or what to do in any way. I will do my best to even keep mere suggestions to an absolute minimum. This is because I am not you, obviously, and therefore could never know what is best for you. Luckily, you can and will.

Also, the combination of perspectives we will be exploring are *descriptive* (about how things work and who you are) as opposed to *prescriptive* (rules for how to behave). There are plenty of books out there professing the supposed "Rules for Life." You don't need another one of those books. Putting forth ten commandments may seem more straightforward, but they would also be generic by default, and based on worn-out assumptions about the nature of the world—and you.

Instead of getting detailed *applications* for each life scenario we will explore in the essays, you will instead be supported in listening to your own innate voice and benefiting from the *implications* of this remembered wisdom.

When you know where to look you'll know what to do.

The Three Principles and Neophytic Non-Duality

It would be close enough to the truth to say the perspectives put forth in this book are a Hodgy-Podgy combination of "The Three

Principles" (also known as the "Inside-Out" paradigm) and what I will call "Neophytic Non-Duality."

The Three Principles

The Three Principles (3Ps) is a paradigm taught by a Scottish dude named Sydney Banks, after experiencing what could be classified as an enlightenment experience. Whether one believes in such experiences, and the seemingly inevitable (and often improbable) "parables" that live on after the founder's death (Syd moved on in 2009), is wholly beside the point.

The point(s) of the 3Ps, if I may be so bold, could be summarized as:

- Thought is the creative force that forms our experience of life moment to moment
- We experience life from the "inside-out," not "outside-in"
- We are not broken, we have simply forgotten and strayed from our home base of innate mental wellness

Section One covers my personal journey, my introduction to the 3Ps, and the impact they have had on my life. You can dig deep into the history and details of the 3Ps in the *Resources for Further Exploration* section.

Non-Duality for Neophytes

ne·o·phyte
/'nēəˌfīt/
a person who is new to a subject, skill, or belief.

(Full disclosure: I include myself in this category; Beginner's Mind for me, all day, every day)

I believe Syd had a "spiritual awakening" and was able to download wisdom from that experience. As often happens, attempts to convey personal spiritual insights to others got tricky, and so many of his students over time created (consciously or otherwise) a *psychology-based* 3P model. This model included language and teaching models more user-friendly and therefore easier to apply to everyday "Relative Reality."

That's cool. After all, it helps to put the 3Ps into the center of our HP Venn Diagram.

But what of the "spiritual" aspect of Syd's experience and message? Or for that matter, what of the freakishly similar experiences and messages of sages throughout history?

And this is where the concept (or *non-concept*, I suppose) of Non-Duality comes into play.

At the most basic level, which is where Truth always resides...

Non-Duality = "not two"

And that's basically it—in an itty, bitty, esoteric nutshell.

Can you get a sense of why this can be such a clusterfuck to talk about?

Although Non-Duality is certainly more esoteric than the Three Principles—and I would even suggest ND is more esoteric than almost any other paradigm—it still has great potential value to us. Sure, Non-Duality addresses the FORMLESS, and I can attest to how easily that can devolve into intellectual masturbation. (For the record, I am NOT against masturbation, intellectual or otherwise.) But at the same time, ND can offer a beautiful depth, a foundational grounding not often visible within the realm of psychology-based teachings and paradigms.

It might be helpful to envision a spectrum: one end is the psychological perspective (3Ps) and the other is spiritual (Non-Duality):

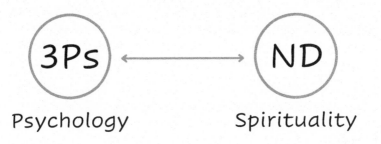

The introduction to Section Five includes as much of a description of the formless element of Non-Duality as I am qualified to put forth, and the subsequent essays will hopefully stoke your own investigation into this perspective and its potential impact on your Being.

How to Read this Book

This diminutive tome is simply a compilation of essays. It is a sharing of where I've been and what I've seen so far. It is a suggestion to look in a particular direction and try it on for size. No need to worry about committing to change your behaviors or your belief systems, or anything else for that matter.

If, like me, your eyes have become strained and tired from diligently seeking and searching, I invite you to relax and simply LOOK.

Look & Ponder.

It has been implied more than twice that I have an inappropriate love of the verb "to ponder." Of course, we know better; nobody has the authority to put love in a corner and deem it inappropriate. Love is always the only answer, regardless of the question.

Pondering is an exploration,
much like contemplation,
but with a smiling smirk
instead of a furrowed brow.

There are many mental positions from which to read a book and differing purposes for doing so: for entertainment, to agree or disagree, for confirmation of one's current beliefs, etc.

You may indeed find portions of this book entertaining, as there's no accounting for good taste. Knock yourself out. However, I humbly request that you humor me by allowing yourself the freedom of steering clear of the compare/contrast, agree/disagree binary mindset that is often the default mode for ingesting new perspectives.

How much can you relax your body, your mind, and even your consciousness while reading a book? Can you read a book in the same way you might listen to music? Can you relax enough to allow the possibility of being impacted?

Can you relax enough to make room for something
fresh,
alive,
new?

I chose the spacing and arrangement of text in this book specifically to encourage you to *Take. It. Slow.* Also, you may be wondering what is up with this funky font?

I chose this hand printed font because it provides more space and, again, invites us to slow down to the speed of life.

It will likely be a change of pace.

Enjoy.

Note 1: There is technically nothing "new" under the sun and certainly not contained within these pages. However, all that is old is new again and, at the very least, we can throw on a fresh coat of paint (insight)—or scrape the old paint away—and perhaps see with new eyes that which has always been there.

Note 2: You will no doubt notice elements of repetition and perhaps even redundancy in the essays and throughout this book. I could play this off as being to your benefit; after all, "repetition is the mother of skill" and such. When all the rhubarb has been harvested, however, it will be clear I am only pointing towards a few simple and potential truths for your consideration, and I am merely a simple man who needs a few simple guideposts.

It's as simple as that.

Layout of Book Sections

In keeping with the relaxed state I'm suggesting to you as the reader, I too have taken this stance with the organization of the book. Although it might serve you well to read the first section first, the downsides for not doing so are minor, and no doubt you'll be able to recover.

So, peruse in whatever manner blows your proverbial skirt up; pick an essay title that sounds inciting and start there, throw the book on the floor and allow it to randomly fall open to a page; or for the more dramatically inclined, set the book ablaze and then urinate on it to douse the flames, reading whatever pages survive the fiery water-sports fetish spectacle. (Disclaimer: Do not try this at home.)

It's all good.

For those who may be unable to perform the latter due to dehydration or just a general sense of appropriateness, and/or who just like to know where we're headed, here's the basic layout:

Section I: Background Check & Basic Training

These initial chapters cover my birth as a seeker and my progressive and on-going quest for "Capital T" Truth and the cessation of seeking.

Section II: People, Culture & Other Profound Annoyances

French philosopher Jean Paul Sartre famously stated, "Hell is Other People." There is no shortage of apparent evidence to support his claim.

Section III: (No) Self Improvement Protocols

Perhaps the best way to care for the Self is to engage in practices pointing to ——> the *absence* of one.

Section IV: Spiritual Enemas

It's time to clean out, get shit moving, and see what remains.

Section V: Neophytic Non-Duality

We will plant a few ND seeds, tackle some "real world" issues/scenarios, and see what sprouts up to nourish us.

Appendix: MetaGnosis Audio Sessions

When experiencing new perspectives, it is often our default to rely solely on our intellect and miss out on the deeper embodied understanding (wisdom) on offer. These audio sessions will encourage you to allow a space to open and further engage your sensory exploration.

Resources for Further Exploration

As a general rule, it is a good idea to hear it from the horse's mouth, and not rely on me talking out of my ass. This is my list of recommended resources from The Three Principles and Non-Dualism stable of thoroughbred teachers and thought leaders.

One Final Note (before I cut you loose)

To be clear, this book is unlikely to change your life, at least directly. I suppose it could plant a few seeds, or water those already within you. It might be a spark that ignites a fire or a gentle breeze that stokes a long dormant ember. I would be both thrilled and honored in either case.

To be clearer, I am not putting this forth as a complete Truth in any way. As a matter of fact, this work is consciously incomplete, because as Quincy Jones famously stated, "When you're making an album you need to make sure you leave some room for God."

And to be clearest, I'm quite aware I'm no Quincy Jones and this book is far from a masterpiece such as Michael Jackson's *Thriller*. That being said, I think leaving some room for God is sage advice; hence the random semi-blank pages throughout. (Feel free to use them for poetry, doodling, rolling a joint and/or drafting a letter of gratitude to your mother or father... it's likely about time, don't ya think?)

My brothers and sisters, family and friends, can you start to smell what I'm stepping in?

Seriously,
come on in,
the water's fine.

Amazon Reviews are the "**Golden Ticket**" for unknown authors.

If you feel compelled, a quick review of my book would be deeply appreciated.

You can use the QR code or link below, or simply search for the book on Amazon.

Thank You!!

https://www.amazon.com/dp/1955821879

SECTION I:
BACKGROUND CHECK &
BASIC TRAINING

CHAPTER ONE:
WHAT IS A GOOD MAN?

"The good man is the friend of all living things."

—Mahatma Gandhi

It was a cautionary tale, of sorts.

I was in my early late teens and 2,301 miles from home.

We had split into breakout groups of ten incoming freshmen and one graduating senior, the idea being that Hank—a name already a few generations past its prime, it occurred to me at the time—would impart to us his six years' worth of hard-earned collegiate wisdom.

It was an open Q & A format, and the first several newbie inquiries were in regards to scheduling classes, specifically the requirement to take a certain number of electives from a category called THE Humanities.

Thankfully, we had Hank.

Hank had a personal tale to tell, one in which a particular Humanities elective was responsible for ravaging his GPA. It was not so subtly implied that the precipitating incident resulted in him now being twenty-four years old and at least one more semester from hurling his graduation cap skyward.

"None of the electives sounded interesting, he said, so after eliminating the ones that sounded horrifically boring, I ended up in *An Introduction to Philosophy: Morals and Ethics.*"

Apparently, it all started out well and good. Although some of the reading material was a bit dense (Plato, Socrates, Kierkegaard etc.), there were no papers to write, and the classes consisted primarily of debates with fellow students on relevant issues of the day. He admitted he found the structure and environment energizing and even... fun. It was his favorite class his first semester.

His propitious relationship with philosophy did an abrupt about-face, however, when he found out about the final exam, which happened to be 100% of his grade. And given the unfamiliar format of the class, it never occurred to Hank to utilize the go-to question he had used with all his high school teachers:

"Will this be on the test?"

Hank recounted the fateful day. "I arrived at the classroom and there was an essay bluebook on each desk. Up on the blackboard was written

'What is a Good Man?'

The graduate student acting as test proctor told us we had two hours."

Perhaps Hank should have majored in Theater, because he delivered this story with a robust amount of heartfelt angst. And it seemed he got the reaction he was going for—shock and horror, at least from the others in the group.

"Yep," he exclaimed, loud enough for members of other breakout groups to hear and take notice, "That's all it said—'What is a good man?' Two hours and a blank notebook for your entire grade. Be friggin' careful with philosophy classes."

Several students in the group were shaking their heads and taking notes. I assumed they were scribbling, "Fuck Philosophy!"

As for me, I too was shocked to hear such a thing.

And utterly enlivened.

Wait—there is a major where I can explore how to become a good man? No shit!

I declared philosophy as my major the next day. Soon thereafter I added psychology and religion, and I was off and running.

A
seeker
was
born.

Save the Wigglies

Truth be told, I sense I was born into this incarnation as a full-on, card-carrying member of The Seeker Society. My realization that I could STUDY such a thing in college was akin to being called up from the minors to the major leagues.

I started "seeking," in one way or another, so early on I likely still reeked of urine.

I was a sensitive kid.

Looking out at the world, I saw things that just didn't seem right, and I felt badly about them. I wanted to be good. I wanted to help, to make things right. This earnest, heart-driven desire gave birth to a cluster of anxiety-ridden OCD behaviors.

One of my more famous became known as "The Rainy-Day Ritual."

I grew up in a traditional suburban neighborhood home with a long blacktop driveway. Any day it had rained, and my family had to drive somewhere, I would PANIC. This was due to my appalling discovery that earthworms would slither from the yard and garden up onto the wet driveway, and subsequently be pulpified by the tires of our car.

I took it upon myself to oversee "wiggly" evacuation and safe relocation. This simply involved picking up the slimy little *lumbricus terrestris* and putting them back into the grass. Being so young, my sense of time was less than accurate, so I often ran out of it. Therefore, I enlisted my younger brother, still in diapers, mind you, to assist me. And when time was especially short, God bless them, my parents would even get in on the project. I can only imagine what the neighbors must have thought, especially on Sundays when we were all dressed up for church.

As we backed out of the driveway and onto the street, the severity of the predicament became clear to me:
all the streets in our hood,
our town, and the whole world
were nothing but killing fields.

So many wigglies,
so little time.

It's somewhat funny and perhaps even—dare I say, endearing—to talk about it now, but I can assure you that at that time, I found the situation, the senseless slaughter of innocent creatures, to be *truly horrifying*. It literally kept me up at night when I could hear the rain outside, anticipating the inevitable carnage, no matter how much I tried to save them.

Did I mention I was a sensitive kid?

As a pre-puber, I admittedly didn't know much about the world, and certainly not the "bigger" issues like war and famine and fascism. So, I mainly focused on non-human animals. But as I got older and into junior high school, I found PLENTY of additional topics to worry about—girls, grades, sports... girls.

To be honest, I was miserable a good deal of the time, and likely would have been diagnosed with an anxiety disorder or depression, if those had been popular labels back then. However, I did have the awareness that my morose sensibilities were out of proportion to my circumstances—I had a lovely home life by any and all standards—and I suffered far more than my friends; they all seemed relatively happy.

I found it quite bewildering.

After much deliberation, I came to what seemed like a logical conclusion—there was something wrong, and it must be something wrong with ME. And it also seemed obvious that all those happy people had something I was missing. So, I had to first figure out what that thing was, and then go out and acquire said unknown thing for myself.

And finally
it occurred to me:
maybe it was just
that good people
got to feel good,
and not-so-good people
got to feel otherwise...

so I had to be "good-er."

My Junior Hero's Journey

I began what you might call my little hero's journey, my attempt to find what I was missing and some way to be a better person... so I would feel better.

I was dedicated to my quest, and so began to study the early pioneers in the Personal Development field, like Norman Vincent Peale. I started doing affirmations and visualizations with more than ample vigor. Later I studied all sorts of techniques like Neuro-linguistic programming (NLP), Cognitive Behavioral Therapy (CBT),

Emotional Freedom Technique (EFT), and dozens of forms of meditation. As previously mentioned, I majored in Philosophy, Psychology, and Religion, and even did some graduate studies in those areas. I found most of these modalities and techniques helpful, and I even taught them to many coaching clients over the years. However, they were a lot of work, and it seemed like none of them worked all the time, especially when I might have needed them the most.

I *knew* I was still missing something. Or so I thought.

That is all to say that, perhaps much like you, I've been there and done that.

Time for something different.

Therefore, we won't be exploring or utilizing any of the "usual suspects" regarding how to feel better. If you've got one or more tools that serve you well, then continue to utilize them to the utmost. I don't feel there is anything wrong with techniques, I've just found them to be limiting and less than 100% reliable.

This also won't be a 10-step program. Everyone seems to like steps, and I get it—if you're on step five, you know you're halfway done. And then when you're on step nine, you're in the home stretch. I guess this approach could be considered a one-step plan, and that step might be off a cliff...

but I'm getting ahead of myself.

You may be wondering... if there aren't steps and there won't be many techniques, what the hell is it we'll be exploring in this book? That's a legit question, and the answer is:

INSIGHTFUL UNDERSTANDING —> WISDOM

What's On Offer?

As I conceded in the introduction, the hodge podge perspective of this book and the essays contained herein utilize a duct-taped-together combination of The Three Principles (The Inside-Out Paradigm), Neophytic Non-Duality, and a big dose of Bhakti-Style Love (Heartful-ness, if you will).

Both of these perspectives and the BS Love are in rather stark contrast to the prevailing paradigm, the popular take on reality, which one could summarize as "Separate and Outside-In."

Two questions for your consideration:

What would it mean to you and the way you navigate your way through life if there was no such thing as an inherently stressful situation, or a fundamentally irritable person, or even a BAD day?

What might it mean for you to realize that you are not a separate entity at odds with the world at large, that there is a grounding of Unity and a bedrock of Peace just below the surface?

I can tell you what it has meant for me and many of my clients... FREEDOM. And not just some specific, minor, or limited element of freedom, like financial freedom, or food freedom or religious freedom; I'm talking about AUTHENTIC FREEDOM, which of course includes all of those elements, but is more foundational and has far broader implications.

This may all sound painfully obtuse, so I promise we'll bring it more down to earth in the next essay—with Teddy Bears, in fact.

Ponder-ables:

What is your definition of a good man, a good woman, or even a good dog?

What has been the trajectory of your journey up to this point?

Have techniques served you well? All the time or some of the time?

Can you sense the potential freedom on offer via insight and wisdom instead of tools and techniques?

CHAPTER TWO:
ADULT TEDDY BEARS

"A teddy bear will give you love. A grizzly bear will give you a mauling. Some bears just aren't the same."
—Anthony T. Hincks

I'm going out on a limb and guessing that one of the more pressing reasons we humans become engaged in any form of personal development or spiritual questing is to feel better.

Are you with me on this?

To that end, we shall now ponder upon the origin of our personal feelings; because without a solid understanding of where they come from, it's challenging to know what they mean and what to do about them.

This essay title was not intentionally deceiving, or in any way meant to be clickbait. "Adult Teddy Bears" does not refer to one of those furry fetishes where consenting adults dress up as animals and do consenting adult things.

Instead, Adult Teddy Bears is a reference to a brilliant metaphor I'm borrowing from one of my mentors, Clarity Coach founder Jamie Smart, which I believe gives us a real-world sense of where our feelings come from, and especially where they DON'T.

You've likely noticed that many toddlers have a teddy bear, other stuffed animals, or maybe a blanket, to which they attribute a great deal of power. They see these inanimate objects as the source of their good feelings, and the absence of them to be cause for feelings of anxiety, insecurity, and unhappiness.

As intelligent grownups, we know the child is innocently mistaken in believing the stuffed animal is somehow "magical," that it has some metaphysical power to create internal feelings in small humans. It's just filled with stuffing, after all.

We know 100% of the good feelings are being created within the child themselves and certainly not from within the teddy bear. This is just an innocent misinterpretation of the origin of their feelings, and it need not be of particular concern for young children.

However, I'm going to suggest this misunderstanding is still quite prevalent regarding Adult Teddy Bears.

As for a few examples, how about your:

Partner
Boss
Money
Health
Past
Future

Am I being so audacious as to suggest that none of these people or circumstances has the power to create a feeling within you? Indeed, I might be that audacious. But I get it—it sure as hell looks that way, doesn't it?

It looks like your partner's behavior is making you upset
or he or she is making you feel loved.

It looks like your boss is making you feel insignificant,
or your fat wallet is making you feel secure.

It looks like waiting on the results of your medical test is making you anxious.

It looks like past successes are making you feel confident today or perhaps your anticipation about some potential future event is making you feel nervous.

I know it looks like these examples have the power to generate feelings within us, both the good feelings and the bad ones.

But I'm putting forth the idea that they're all

Adult
Teddy
Bears.

The Myth of Stressful Situations

Let's take the example of "stressful jobs." It's well accepted in most parts of the world that some jobs are inherently stressful. This would imply the job itself directly causes the feelings of stress within people performing the job.

Fair enough, maybe...

But what about the fact that not everyone experiences the same amount of stress, or even any stress at all, while doing the same job? If a job was inherently stressful, then 100% of people would feel stressed while doing it.

According to a 2019 survey, the top stressful jobs in the US were:

1) Military Personnel
2) Firefighter
3) Air Traffic Controller

Although it is likely most people working

in those professions would classify their work as "stressful," I can assure you it is not 100%, as I've met people within two of those professions that find their work "calming," "meditative," or even "Zen-like."

If indeed it were the external environment causing the internal feelings of stress, wouldn't it make sense that everyone would feel stressed, even if it varied a bit in intensity? However, there are people who feel the *opposite* of stress in these supposedly stressful environments.

The variable is within each individual person.

The nature of all situations is *inherently neutral.*

We humans are engaged within these situations and have thoughts about them. These thoughts then generate feelings.

Feelings are Shadows of Thought

We experience our THINKING, not the external WORLD.

What we are thinking at the present moment can even create feelings about our future. As an example, let's say you have a public speaking engagement next month. If you are feeling anxious, it seems as though it's because of that future event.

However, I would suggest those feelings are not about the upcoming event, it's because you are having anxious thoughts in this present moment. Your feelings aren't telling you anything about

YOU
or
the
EVENT.

Consider how absurd it sounds when we break it down—the idea that a future event somehow causes a present moment feeling.

Here you are, in the present moment, and there is the possibility of you giving a presentation in a few weeks. There is no guarantee it will happen, of course; nobody knows the future for sure, but it's on the calendar. So, for this to work, the potential event would need to be a "thing," which it's not, at least not yet. That "thing" would somehow have to travel back in time to the present day, inhabit your body, and then generate the feelings of anxiousness.

Come on, that is some crazy science fiction shit right there!

We experience our thinking, not the external world. Our thoughts are generating our feelings, moment to moment to moment.

This is great news, by the way, and I can attest to the freedom right there at your fingertips when you gain a broader perspective of *how things actually work.*

In the next essay, we'll explore why even though feelings are only generated by thoughts, feelings can still provide valuable information and can pave the way for insightful understanding.

Ponder-ables:

Can you get a sense that, no matter how much this looks like other people or circumstances dictate how we feel in the moment, there is something else at play?

And can you sense that the "middleman" is thought?

What are your most real-looking adult teddy bears?

Can you sense the beautiful freedom available when one is liberated from the victimhood of external circumstances?

CHAPTER THREE: YOUR FECAL-COLORED FEELINGS

Poop isn't my absolute favorite subject for spiritual jokes and metaphors, butt it's a solid number two.

If the kind of thoughts we're having at any given moment determine the kind of feelings we're feeling... then why don't we just make sure we're always having positive, happy thoughts?

It will be all rainbows and unicorns, maybe even rainbow-pooping unicorns.

Makes perfect sense.

Easy-Peasy,
Lemon-Squeezy.

Who among us hasn't done a "positive thinking program"? I've used this type of strategy many times, and it can be somewhat effective, at least sometimes. But if you're anything like me—God help you if you're too much like me—you've likely noticed two things:

1) Positive Thinking doesn't always work, and seems to fail when you MOST need it

2) Even when it does work, it can be a helluva lot of work.

I had taken on the role of the *Thought Police* and was on constant high alert. Each incoming thought had to be monitored and categorized:

GOOD Thoughts: OK, these are permitted and should be encouraged as well as preserved

NEUTRAL Thoughts: Uncertain, and likely to be context-dependent

BAD Thoughts: These need to be expelled from our brain and kept at bay

Have you noticed that these "Bad Thoughts" are the most persistent, and that they seem to breed like rabbits?

Thoughts & Feelings— What Are They Good For?

Where do thoughts come from?

Nobody truly knows. Scientists make up hypotheses, because that's what they're paid to do, but when pressed, they will admit they're clueless. Thoughts seem to come out of the ether sometimes, don't they? We all have brilliant thoughts in the shower (more on that later) and we all have crazy thoughts at the most random times.

I've had seven thoughts today that if acted on would earn me some serious time in a crowbar hotel, and it isn't even noon yet.

Here's the thing: if we're going to attempt to control our incoming thoughts (as in positive thinking protocols), it seems that knowing their origin would be useful, and seeing we don't...well, good luck with that.

What do Feelings mean?

Feelings drive most of our behaviors (if we allow them such influence), so knowing what they mean could be considered crucial information.

I'd like to put forth an analogy for your consideration: your thoughts at any given moment are sunglasses of various colors, as in "seeing the world through rose-colored glasses."

What if your feelings ONLY informed you of the color/shade of your current "thought sunglasses"?

Nothing more, nothing less; that would be the *entirety* of their meaning.

For example, we've all woken up wearing rose-colored glasses. A day when everything felt easy, even things that normally would have felt epically hemorrhoidal. That annoying guy at work—he means well and can be kinda cute, even when he farts all the time. Stuck in gridlock on the freeway—what a great time to call and catch up with friends and family.

These are pleasant glasses to wear. Life is good.

But then we've also experienced waking up on the wrong side of the web, wearing fecal-colored glasses that make everything look like turd soup. I mean, you could be lovingly mobbed by golden retriever puppies and get pissed about the dog hair on your clothes.

I am suggesting that your feelings in the moment are a perfect indication of one thing and one thing only—the color of your current thought glasses. They can't tell you a damn thing about you, anyone else, the situation you find yourself in, the past, or about your future...

It's
Just
The
Glasses.

Furthermore, have you noticed you don't wear the same color glasses all the time, that somehow, someway, they get switched out... one minute you're upset and then ten minutes later you feel better?

State Manipulation vs. State Awareness

Most people prefer the rose-colored glasses over the fecal-colored ones. Life is a bit more enjoyable that way. And that's *exactly* what I was trying to do for over thirty years, figure out how to master "emotional state manipulation."

I thought if I could do that... I'd have FREEDOM.

All those techniques, tools and tricks allowed me (usually/sometimes) to be able to change the color of my thought glasses in the moment. If I was feeling anxious, and I wanted to feel confident instead, I would re-frame this, double disassociate that, tap an EFT point, do some naked yoga or whatever, and *Voilà*... my glasses would get swapped out, upgraded.

It felt like freedom, but then I got this inkling...

Ink·ling
/'iNGkliNG/
noun
a slight knowledge or suspicion; a hint.

(note to self: always follow your inklings)

Maybe being "here" and needing to be over "there" might not be freedom after all.

Even though I was confident that having preferences was part of being human, having to have my preferences met, right this minute, and the belief there was somewhere better to be (a better emotional state)...

...it began to smell like a cheap knock-off of freedom.

Over time I've come to appreciate that it's *not* the ability to manipulate my emotional states that is the origin of freedom, but rather the simple AWARENESS that I'm always wearing thought glasses, and I'll be wearing a different colored pair sooner or later, usually sooner, whether I do anything or not. And THAT is where the juice of authentic freedom can be squeezed and savored.

You may be questioning how simple *awareness* of our mental state is cooler than being able to *manipulate* our mental state.

What makes awareness so valuable?

Fair enough.

Here's an example from Transformative Coach Michael Neill:

Let's say you're patronizing a local bar on a Saturday night. There's a good chance you'll run across some inebriated individuals. Imagine there are two such people with about the same body weight and alcohol tolerance, and both are snot-slinging drunk. The only difference is, one of them knows they are seriously impaired (he has an awareness of his state) and the other does not. Which one do you think is *more dangerous*?

The drunk person who knows they are drunk at least has the option of making an informed decision. They know they are impaired, therefore (hopefully) they will choose not to drive themselves home. This can literally be a life-and-death matter for themselves and others. The other person, who lacks the awareness, doesn't even have the option of choosing.

Awareness & Insights

Awareness is so vital because it leads us towards, and sets up the conditions for, *Insightful Understanding.*

Once we understand *How Things Work*, manipulating our emotional state loses much of its appeal. As a matter of fact, it often seems unnecessary because we begin to experience the same circumstances differently anyway.

For example, if you were young enough when you first watched *The Wizard of OZ*, those flying blue monkeys likely scared the bejesus out of you. However, once you understood how movies and television worked, that the scary images were just light and shadows dancing on a screen, you no longer had any fear. You didn't need a methodology or technique (or therapy) to overcome your fear; the embodied, insightful understanding of how things worked was enough to change your blue monkey relationship permanently.

Ponder-ables:

Have you employed a positive thinking protocol on your self-development journey? What results have you experienced?

What might it mean for you, if indeed it were true, that your current feelings are a direct result of your current thoughts, and nothing else?

What is your favorite poop joke?

CHAPTER FOUR:
THE END OF WORRY
(THREE STEPS TO LESS STRESS)

"Worry is preposterous. We don't know enough to worry."
— Terrence McKenna

Let's talk about stress, baby, you and me.

There are many kinds of stress, and not all of them are detrimental. For example, my wife and I own a holistic health and fitness studio, and an integral part of our members' programs is strength training, which is a form of physical stress. Strength training creates micro-tears in the muscles, damaging them in an intentionally stressful way. We help them to strategically stress their bodies so they can rest and repair and come back stronger and more resilient.

You could also say that educating yourself, learning new things, is a form of intellectual stress, with the payoff being increased knowledge. Those are two examples of stress that can be good for you when utilized in the proper dosages.

It's a bit of a different story when it comes to mental/emotional stress. It has become evident in recent years that too much of this kind of stress can

literally
kill
us.

So, what are we to do?

Let's keep our eye on the prize (insight) that the origin of mental/ emotional stress is *thought*. And stressful feelings, like all feelings, are simply the product of *thought in the moment*. There aren't any *inherently* stressful circumstances or people, there are only stressful thoughts, which in turn lead to stressful feelings.

I've got some good news
and some potentially bad news.

The good news is once you embody this perspective, not just intellectually, but when you know and feel it to be true deep within your bones, it will all start to fall into place, and it's just a matter of time. And by all, I do mean everything. And by time, well, I have no idea, I'm not the boss of time. But you can rest assured when you look in the direction of Truth, you'll see what you're ready to see, whenever that may be.

Now, the potentially bad news: if you're keen on constantly hearing new concepts and perspectives... I've pretty much blown my wad here already...

YOU ARE LIVING
IN THE FEELING OF YOUR THINKING,
NOT IN THE FEELING
OF YOUR CIRCUMSTANCES.

That really is the long and the short of it. I could (perhaps even *should*) leave it at that.

As they say, "Why shear a pig?"

That being said, there's actually fleece on this here pig, as well as a lot more to this perspective than might appear at first glance. Rather, it's that the implications of this understanding run deep and wide. This paradigm shift certainly has the capacity to change your life. But I want to be clear about the kind of changes that are on offer.

Insightful Understanding doesn't directly change your external circumstances, but it absolutely affects how you interpret those circumstances.

Insightful Understanding reminds you *how things work*, specifically how your mind works, but everything else as well.

For example, I prefer sunny days over cloudy days. On a cloudy day, I don't panic that the sun isn't there, that maybe it's burned out and life as we know it is doomed. I know enough about clouds, and I've had enough experience to know the sun is still there, behind the clouds, and that it will be out again sooner or later. But understanding *how clouds work* doesn't make them dissipate or move on any faster. It just means I don't have to stress about the end of the world.

One less thing to worry about.

What to Do When You are Worried or Stressed Out

There are many among us, including yours truly, who occasionally find it challenging to fully let go of worry because we think it is useful in some regard; it keeps us safe.

Reminds me of this little ditty of a parable:

A police officer is called to the village square because, as odd as it might seem, there is a man on the pavilion who is twirling a tiger by the tail over his head.

The police officer cautiously approaches the man and inquires as to what the hell he's doing and why. The man responds, "This keeps the lions away."

The officer informs him there aren't any lions in town, to which man responds

"See, it's working!"

I've got some more good news for you. Your meat suit is designed with lots of self-correcting, self-healing mechanisms... lots and lots. They're not even mechanisms— they're entire networks of systems. And they come standard with the human body.

For example, what happens when you get a minor scrape or cut?

I'm no doctor, but I do know our bodies go to work immediately to heal it. All sorts of immune cells rush in, blood flow slows down, macrophages start to clean up, new tissue cells are built, and remodeling occurs. It's an amazing process. Now, what do you have to do to make all of that happen?

Nothing, Nada, Zilch.

What's the main thing you can do to screw it up?

Pick at the scab!

When you pick at a scab, you interfere with the natural healing system and often delay it, sometimes even causing an infection.

Another simple example is digestion. If you've eaten recently, your body is in the process of digestion, without you needing to monitor it. Your body self-regulates that on your behalf. I suppose you could interfere with your digestion by drinking a bottle of hot sauce (this is an obtuse analogy, not a recommendation), which seems like the equivalent of picking the scab of digestion.

Our Psychological Immune System

There are many other examples of self-healing and regulatory systems within our bodies. Why the hell would our psychological system be designed differently? Why wouldn't it also be self-regulating? That wouldn't make a damn bit of sense, now, would it?

Maybe you can easily get on board with the wound healing and digestion examples, but you're a bit skeptical and don't feel as though you can trust your psychological immune system to kick into gear when you need it.

Let me guess—you'd like a step-by-step process to activate this self-correcting mental wellness system.

As I've already stated, I tend to avoid giving multiple step directives much like I avoid bedbugs. There are just so many "Three Steps to Six Pack Abs" or "Five Steps to $10,000 a Month" programs being peddled to us these days; it all just seems silly.

However, my clients *constantly* ask me for steps, and as three steps seems to be the minimum, I'm going to acquiesce here and do just that.

Here are *The Three (Non) Steps to Less Stress* via activation of your innate mental wellness system:

1) Notice
2) Calm The Fuck Down (CTFD)
3) Do NOTHING (Don't pick at the scab)
   Note: Doing nothing doesn't always mean no action at all is taken, just like emptiness isn't empty and silence isn't silent. More on this soon.

I am well aware those are somewhat backhanded steps, or at least they may look that way. To be fair, I did call them *Non*-Steps. Let's look at each of them one by one in the next three essays.

Ponder-ables:

Can you remember a personal example of discovering *how something worked* (insightful understanding) that resulted in a dramatic and instant change in your relationship to said thing?

Can you sense how your mental/emotional

states vary over time, but sooner or later come back towards homeostasis?

What are the "scabs" you find challenging *not* to pick?

CHAPTER FIVE:
ON NOTICING &
PURE AWARENESS

"I noticed that you are not noticing me."

Step number one is to simply *notice*.

What does that mean and how does one do it?

The mind as a snow globe is a popular metaphor in the Transformative Coaching world. Picture your mind as a snow globe: sometimes it gets shaken up and creates a small blizzard, making it hard to see what's really going on inside. If we attempt to settle the snow by shaking the globe, it only makes it worse. When left alone, the snow naturally settles, and there is a clearer view and a more tranquil setting.

Noticing simply points towards the *awareness* of our mental state moment to moment. Not judging it or trying to change it. Most people move in and out of their internal blizzards and tranquil states many times throughout a day, but they don't notice these shifts taking place. I've yet to meet a client who is truly *always* stressed out, in a blizzard state all the time. They certainly may feel that way, but upon further inspection, they do indeed have periods of tranquil mental states as well.

It can be helpful to notice the transient nature of these two seemingly opposing states, and all the ones in between. As soon as we truly recognize their constant comings and goings, we tend to take them less seriously.

But I may be getting ahead of myself.

How and What to Notice

First and foremost, I encourage people to feel their feelings, whether they be rose-colored or hideous shades of fecal matter; that's what the hell they're there for, after all.

After an acknowledgment and the felt sense of said feelings, *notice your narrative*. What is the story you are attaching to these feelings? We've already looked into the mistaken conclusion that the origin of our feelings is anyone or anything external to ourselves. But what about the stories that we so eagerly create about what these feelings must mean?

Notice that your narrative is composed entirely of *thought* material. Your thoughts elicited your current feelings and now thoughts about those thought-created feelings are creating your story.

It is simply a matter of noticing how much we are up in our own heads—or, as it often is in my case, how far my head is up my ass.

This is when a shift can be allowed to occur, from

Noticing
to
Witnessing
Awareness.

This may be viewed as an unnecessary distinction, linguistic masturbation even. (I've been accused of much worse, I assure you.) But I stand by it.

Try this on for size/take this out for a ride:

As you begin to notice your feelings and then your narrative, you will also be able to *notice yourself noticing* these sensations and the internally created stories. This noticing of yourself noticing is called *Witness Awareness.*

The Witness Awareness State can be a valuable tool on your journey. It might be considered a first level disassociation, but not in a troubling or escapist way. Rather, it can provide enough space to see more of what is truly happening moment to moment and continue your inquiry deeper and deeper.

There are states of Awareness that, for lack of a better term, are *beyond* the Witness State.

The State of Pure Awareness

I am going to use the term "Pure Awareness" here, not because this state is necessarily "better" than the Witness State or any other, but simply for the purposes of useful differentiation.

Unlike within Witness Awareness, where one can see/watch/sense oneself having experiences, in the State of Pure Awareness, the identity of Self is gone—transcended, if you will.

These states might also be delineated by the terms "Self-Conscious" and "Self-Awareness." (I am taking liberties with these definitions and molding them for my purposes—so sue me.)

When one is "Self-Conscious," which one can be while abiding in the Witness State, the question may well occur "How am I doing?" Or more specifically, "How is the one that I am watching doing?" Again, this can be useful and productive on our evolutionary journey.

However, when I use the term "Self-Awareness," I am pointing to a state in which there is no Self; a state in which a question such as "How am I doing?" wouldn't make any sense.

In essence, this is because you recognize, at some level, that you are Awareness itself.

This is also a key characteristic of the "flow state" or being "in the zone" that we often hear about in relation to athletes and other high-level performers, although we all enter into and out of such states frequently. This is a state in which we "lose ourselves" as we become absorbed in our work or play, and often experience time distortion. (It speeds up or slows down.)

The Silence of Pure Awareness

The State of Pure Awareness, by virtue of lacking an individual, separate self, is one of internal silence.

It is also a state of peace.

But not by effort—rather by design.

The silent space of Pure Awareness is the passageway, the first (and only necessary) step towards a solution to any problem, as all problems are composed of thoughts relating to the illusory separate self-identity.

This limited sense of self is the origin of all stress. When this drops away within the State of Pure Awareness, it creates a space where your Innate Wisdom can emerge.

Note: We will take a header/faceplant into the illusory, separate self-quandary and its many implications in Section V: Neophytic Non-Duality.

Ponder-ables:

What happens when you step back a bit and notice what it is you are feeling?

And then when you step back further, to the Witness State, can you watch yourself having the experience?

Who is it that is watching?

Try double disassociating—see if you can watch yourself watching yourself having the experience.

Can you sense there is a state of *Pure Awareness* beyond any idea of watching that which makes up "you"?

Can you feel the silence and peace of that space?

CHAPTER SIX:
HOW TO CALM THE
FUCK DOWN

"Never in the history of calming down has anyone ever calmed down by being told to calm down."

I'm not what anyone would confuse for a "how to" coach. Partially because the dermis and feline can be divorced by manifold methods, and with technology these days there are more ways to find out *how to do something/anything* than ever before; likely too many.

Keep in mind our distinction—

Implication
vs.
Application

I sometimes get a rap as the "Anti-Technique Coach." To be clear, I'm not "anti" anything, except maybe olives. I can't stand olives.

If you've got tools, techniques, rituals or what have you, that assist you in calming the fuck down, then please utilize them. This includes meditation, hypnosis, visualization, affirmations, yoga, pranayama or other breathing methods, journaling, tapping, NLP, CBT, whatever.

You will even find a few tools for your perusal in the *Appendix: MetaGnosis Audio Sessions*.

Tools and techniques are not inherently problematic. The issue is when people get confused into believing there is something "magical" about their technique du jour, that without it they'd be lost, that the calm state they seek is *only* to be found through that particular practice, instead of it simply providing an advantageous set and setting, making it a bit easier to allow that desired state to arise from within you.

Putting techniques aside for the moment, let's chat for a spell about calming our asses down via a *foundational understanding* because (and I will gladly die on this hill), understanding is *always* more reliable than tools and techniques.

The "Fucked Up Four" Cycle

In exploring this aspect of foundational understanding, we will ponder upon

Insecurity
Worry
Fear

and Control.

I propose that *but for our thoughts*—peace, serenity and calmness is our default state. That means it's not so important to learn *how* to calm down as it is to recognize how it is that we disengage from our home base enough to get "all hot and bothered" in the first place.

I will further propose that the primary reason we get pulled off our home base is *insecurity*.

When I get insecure about something in the external world, I feel the need to take some action, to change or control whatever that external thing may be—a person or the circumstances. It is easy to fall for the classic "Outside-In Misunderstanding"—my internal feeling state is caused by someone or something "out there."

When feeling insecure, we humanoids tend to succumb to *worry*, which preoccupies our minds and distracts us from the present moment. Not only that, but we're also grand creators of stories, often catastrophic ones— have you noticed?—and we mistake worry for *fear*, which we then feel is legitimate because it keeps us safe.

Which then leads to what I would classify as the world's top fetish—CONTROL.

Let's take a closer look at each of these elements—worry, fear and control—and the truthfulness and usefulness of each.

First, there is an important distinction between worry and fear. Fear is our body's true protective, survival response to clear and present danger. For most of us, it will be a rare occurrence in your lives. When real, clear, and present danger is faced, your body goes into overdrive and pumps adrenaline throughout your system... you're ready to ACT! It's a damn good design and we should all be glad we have it built in, and that we rarely must utilize it.

But here's the rub: we tend to act as if we have imminent dangers lurking around every corner. Even though our bodies don't react with a full-on fear state activation, our minds ruminate with, you guessed it... worry. We perceive all sorts of threats and feel, often subconsciously, that this worrying has at least some value. It feels shitty, but it also can feel like it is keeping us safe, on guard, and alert to what could go wrong.

And that's where we get confused. Worrying acts to dull our perceptions, it preoccupies our minds and clouds access to our innate wisdom.

Of course, we can all come up with examples from the past where it *seemed* as though worrying paid off. Recall the guy twirling a tiger by the tail tale from Chapter Four?

As we begin to trust that our bodies are designed to respond appropriately to fear in the rare instances where it's needed, we can see that all the other low-grade, fear-like feelings we experience are just worry; not real and certainly not helpful.

How do you circumvent your worrisome feelings? I wouldn't worry about it. As you begin to see the structure, order of operations, and the innocent misunderstanding of what they mean, worrisome feelings naturally start to dissipate.

Finally, onto *control*.

The desire to control the external world, and the worrying we perpetuate because that's impossible, is what separates us from our natural state of peace and tranquility.

Control
is the
antithesis
of
authentic
freedom.

The illusion of control we buy into provides a false sense of security. You do have a true foundational security, but it sure as hell isn't to be found within control. If you believe that in the past you've been able to control things and you've based your security upon that illusion, then when you encounter a situation that makes the falsity of this belief abundantly clear, the excrement will no doubt hit the rotatory impellers.

Once we recognize we *never* had control, and things *always* work out (one way or other) we can naturally, effortlessly start to relax, Calm the Fuck Down, and simply put one foot in front of the other knowing the path will unfold beneath our feet.

Ponder-ables:

Have you ever been in clear and present danger? How did your body/mind react?

Can you sense how easy it can be to confuse true danger with thought-generated worry?

When have you twirled a tiger by the tail, attempting to keep something from happening?

What if our control fetish is the only illusory lock on the gateway to our authentic freedom?

CHAPTER SEVEN:
THE ART OF DOING NOTHING

"You do not need to leave your room. Remain sitting at your table and listen. Do not even listen, simply wait, be quiet, still and solitary. The world will freely offer itself to you to be unmasked, it has no choice, it will roll in ecstasy at your feet."
—Franz Kafka

Now that we have taken notice and allowed ourselves to calm the fuck down (and *allowing* is the operative word), let's move onto the art of "doing nothing."

As I previously confessed, although I've had a bit of formal education and will occasionally spit out a ten-dollar word like "ontological," truth be told—I am a simple man.

So simple, in fact, that a full half of my hodge podge adopted paradigm (The 3Ps or The Inside-Out Understanding), as previously stated, can be summarized as follows:

We are living in the feeling of our thinking, not the feeling of our circumstances.

Feelings only tell us about the consciousness

level of our current thinking. The self-evident fact that all thoughts are transient means their resulting feelings also have a shelf life, often shorter than we imagine. Feelings tend to move through us unless we grab hold of them and feed them with our attention, but even then, they will vaporize at some point and new thoughts will emerge.

It's as simple as that.

I tend to be obnoxiously verbose, so it could be simplified further still:

We feel what we think,
and as our thinking changes,
so do our feelings.

Hello new thought,
and hello new feeling.

Let's be real for a minute. You already KNOW this to be true at some level. But—and this is a big butt and I cannot lie—here's the thing: when something is so obvious, so normal, it can become somewhat invisible, and once invisible, it's easy to lose the interconnected causal relationship between all the elements of life.

What does it mean to "Do Nothing"?

There are many spiritual traditions, and some purely secular programs, that have a "do nothing" protocol. These are often evoked to highlight the lesson that we don't have to react to any particular scenario in any particular way.

For example, I spent a couple of decades practicing Zen Buddhism, which involved a strict discipline of seated meditation. As I was taught, you sat your ass down with perfect posture, your hands just-so, and you didn't move for one hour. PERIOD. If you had back pain, or you felt as though your ACL was beginning to tear off the bone from being cranked unnaturally into the lotus position, so be it. And there were interesting lessons to be learned. Oftentimes, focusing on the pain diminished it; sometimes the pain moved around the body.

It was fascinating, indeed.

That is, until one day when I was only 20 minutes into a session and a wasp landed on my inner thigh and proceeded to navigate its way under my shorts (it was an outdoor meditation on the beaches of California, hence the informal attire). The little bastard eventually stung my berry basket. I wish I could report how I channeled my inner Chuck Norris and hardly noticed... but

I flipped out. So much for not needing to react. That was the theory. But as they say, "The difference between theory and practice is that in theory there is no difference." So even though I failed to be nonreactive in this case, the key is the value of the *pause* between stimulus and response, and it is within that space we have *choice*.

It's a fine perspective and can be quite useful. Check it out and see how it serves you.

However, it's not exactly what I'm pointing towards with my "doing nothing" third step. Instead, I'm suggesting that there is rarely anything to be done, at least in relation to your thought-generated feelings. Not only are your feelings mere shadows of your thoughts, but your entire internal experience of the "external" world is self-created by thought. We've made it all up, believed it to be real, and then we have reacted to it, usually attempting to fix it in some fashion or another.

We don't need to do that. And when we are conscious of the nature of the game, it just doesn't seem to make as much sense.

This is not to say you shouldn't go out into the world and do shit; or even as an old mentor Tony Robbins would proclaim, "Take Massive Action." The key, I believe, is to recognize when you are in a more centered place, instead of being caught up in a thought-blizzard, and from there feel your way to taking action, of whatever magnitude, or not.

The Art of Sailing vs. Rowing

There is a principle in Taoism called Wu Wei.

"Wu" is translated as "no or non," and Wei is often translated as "action."

Alan Watts warned that to interpret Wu Wei as a lazy or passive approach would be an error. Instead, Watts defined Wei as "forcing," so Wu Wei would be "not forcing."

Watts explained that to be in line with the Tao is to be in accordance with the flow of life itself.

Within the Ocean of Being, it is the difference between the *art* of sailing and the *effort* of rowing.

The Room of Ten Thousand Demons

If I were to give advice, which I never do, it would be much in line with the famous Zen tale, "The Room of Ten Thousand Demons."

It goes something like this:

There is a room carved into the mountainside of a great monastery in Tibet, known as The Room of Ten Thousand Demons. Once every century, the senior monks open the monastery and invite those looking for a quick hack to attain enlightenment.

The rules are quite simple.

Once you enter the room, the door locks behind you. There is another door a short distance away, and all you must do is walk over to the door and pass through it to attain enlightenment.

The challenge is that these damn ten thousand demons can read your mind and project your darkest fears into the room with you. Whatever you fear most, such as blood or clowns or spiders, the room will be engulfed with those things. For me, I have Anatidaephobia (the fear that somewhere in the world, a duck or goose is watching me). It's a real thing and would likely be the weirdest scenario the demons have ever conjured up.

Even though it's only a short walk to the other side of the room and the doorway to enlightenment, most seekers get so paralyzed by their thought-generated fears that they perish in the room.

The monks offer only two bits of advice to those seekers entering the room:

1) *Whatever you see is purely a reflection of your own thoughts (AKA the Inside-Out Understanding)*

and

2) *Whatever you see or feel, just keep your feet moving*

I like that. There's nothing you can do about your thoughts or feelings, but that shouldn't stop you from moving towards your own awakening and returning to your innate well-being.

Ponder-ables:

What if you felt free to feel all your feelings without feeling compelled to act on them?

Can you appreciate the difference between rowing and sailing; between forcing and moving with just the right amount of effort, and allowing the flow to move you?

What would you have the demons project from your fear library as you began your trek across The Room?

Do you find yourself in The Room on a regular basis?

SLOW

DOWN

SECTION ii:
PEOPLE, CULTURE & OTHER PROFOUND ANNOYANCES

CHAPTER EIGHT:
THE ART OF FORGIVENESS &
PSYCHOLOGICAL INNOCENCE

I asked God for a bike, but I know God doesn't work that way. So, I stole a bike and asked God for forgiveness.

-Emo Philips

According to 3P legend, the first time Syd Banks spoke at a prison, he began his talk by flinging his arms wide and declaring to the assembled group, "You are all innocent."

This excited the inmates and caused a bit of apprehension among the staff. He went on to explain that we all have psychological innocence because:

"Every human being is doing the best they can, given the thinking they have that looks real to them."

Psychologically, we are all innocent.

All
the
time.

Let's ponder on this one for a minute.

Some real-life contexts might be helpful to assist us in this endeavor: Meet my client Carol (not her real name, obviously).

Carol had been married for two years, and it all seemed to be going swimmingly. That was until her husband started two-timing her with the checkout woman at the Piggly Wiggly, lied to her about it for months, and then eventually fessed up. He apologized profusely and has sworn to be the world's best hubby from now until the end of time. Although she feels he is being sincere, she is having a tough time forgiving him.

Is he psychologically innocent? Should Carol forgive him? Should she remain in the relationship?

Let me start with a few initial thoughts, followed by *a multitude* of caveats. Life is like that sometimes. There is an ultimate Truth, but also an infinite number of caveats (plus, I love me some caveats).

Just the Facts

Carol is hurt and confused about how to handle her feelings. She has been studying the 3P paradigm, and she "gets it" (at least intellectually)—nobody can do anything to hurt her feelings. She says, "I know it's just my thinking about what he did, and I should forgive him. I'm just finding it difficult to do."

The husband lied, and then he apologized. The act of him lying in no way can cause her to feel badly, or any way at all for that matter. Although there seems to be a strong correlation between his act and her feelings, it is a false causal relationship. It is her thoughts that occur in reaction to his actions that are the true cause of her feelings.

In other words,
it is her painful thinking
creating her painful emotions.

Fair enough.

Now for a few crucial caveats:

Caveat One:

Feelings are real.

As the memes implore you these days, "Feel All the Feels." Having feelings is a defining characteristic of being human. The fact is, they ebb and flow. Sometimes we have shitty feelings and sometimes we experience ecstasy. That's the nature of the game. Experiencing life through being human is the best game in town, at least at this level of consciousness, at least as far as I know at this point.

Play the damn game!

Experience and respect your feelings. My one suggestion: keep in mind that most of us get off track by forgetting that our feelings are simply shadows of our current thoughts. We take our feelings to mean something else and attribute their origin to other people or our circumstances—present, past and even future.

Caveat Two:

It is unwise and devoid of compassion to tell someone, including yourself, "It's just your thinking." Although technically true (but not fully accurate), it's just rarely useful.

It is not fully accurate because—and this may well sound like linguistic jujitsu bullshit—it's not JUST your thinking, it's simply THAT you're thinking.

You think, I think, we all think, it's what our minds do. However, thoughts and their accompanying feelings are designed to flow through us, and they will. How long that ride lasts depends on several variables, the most influential one being whether we grab hold of said thoughts and associated feelings.

There's nothing wrong with taking a ride. It's just nice to remember you have the option to disembark at any time.

Again,
it's NOT
just your thinking;
it's simply *that you think.*

Psychological Innocence

The basis of psychological innocence is that everyone is *always* doing what makes sense to them in the moment, given the thinking, and the associated feelings, they take to BE REAL and TRUE.

That is to say, their level of thought consciousness in the moment will determine their actions or inactions. People only and always do what makes sense to them moment to moment. To expect anyone to do otherwise is to ask them to be insane.

Of course, we've all done things and then thought later (maybe seconds later, maybe decades later) ...

"What the hell
was I thinking?"

And that's the *perfect* question, because it was indeed the thinking that looked real in that moment that predicated our action.

Everyone is bound to do whatever looks real to them in the moment.

And in that regard, we are all psychologically innocent for any and all of our actions.

Caveat Three:

That is NOT to say people shouldn't be held accountable for their actions.

There are consequences for certain behaviors, and sometimes that could mean disengaging from a personal or professional relationship with them or even putting someone in prison to protect the physical well-being of others within society.

Carol has every right to decide that her husband's behavior is not compatible with the kind of relationship she desires, and to dump his ass. To be clear, even though he is "psychologically innocent," and even though his actions are NOT the cause of her hurt feelings, it is her independent right to choose to spent time with him in the future, or not.

Freedom

If Carol decides to end the relationship, how has this understanding benefited her?

What's at stake here for Carol, whether she stays with her husband or not, is her *freedom*.

As Carol sees clearly how her mind works, she is no longer an emotional victim of circumstance. She not only stops blaming others for how she feels, she has empathy for their humanness. And without blame, the whole concept of forgiveness starts to lose meaning. It is only from a position of victimhood that one attempts to forgive others.

The reason *freedom* is at the foundation of this understanding is because it is purely *descriptive*, not *prescriptive*. It suggests *how things work;* the role of our minds and our experiences of relative reality, but in no way implies what you should do with that understanding and the resulting freedom.

Just because Carol comes to see that her husband didn't cause her hurt feelings, and that he is psychologically innocent, it doesn't mean *therefore* that she has to stay in the relationship...

There is no
THEREFORE
in this paradigm,
and that's exactly
how it creates
FREEDOM.

When you know where to look, when you know how things work, you know what to do... whatever makes the most sense in the moment.

Ponder-ables:

Can you sense the freedom available to us when we understand the origin of all behavior—simply thoughts and the associated feelings seeming real in the moment?

What if forgiveness was automatic, or even better, was no longer a meaningful concept at all?

This inclusive psychological innocence (and forgiveness) is to be extended to ourselves as well.

CHAPTER NINE: BUMPERSTICKER PHILOSOPHERS

*"Out beyond ideas of wrongdoing
and right-doing there is a field.
I'll meet you there.
When the soul lies down in that grass
the world is too full to talk about."*

—*Rumi*

It has been suggested, on more than a few occasions, that I have an Obsessive-Compulsive Disorder regarding bumper sticker analysis, among other topics.

It's not untrue that I may have spent more than what might seem a reasonable amount of time analyzing the literal and figurative meanings of such rear end declarations and the intent of the driver in communicating said messages to whomever is unfortunate enough to find themselves on their caboose end of traffic.

Bumper stickers are a half-ass commitment, as they're a pain in the ass to remove. Not a full-ass commitment, such as a tattoo on your virgin epidermis, but more serious than an easily removed window decal.

It seems there are several reasons drivers may be inclined to decorate their boots:

1) To fly their freak flag, i.e., *Keep Austin Weird*
2) Declare their membership within a group or tribe, i.e., *Vietnam Veteran, Gay Men's Choir*
3) Attempt to influence or persuade, i.e., *Vote Dem or Republican, Look Twice for Motorcycles*
4) Humor—I drive a SMART car. You know, those pseudo-cars about as big as the little end of nothing. People have driven over me believing my car to be a speed bump. My bumper sticker reads
I killed the clowns and stole their car.

The Persuasive Power of Bumper Stickers

Can a bumper sticker truly impact another person's beliefs and/or behavior?

I'm inclined towards skepticism, but one personal experience suggests otherwise.

When I was 14 years old, a bumper sticker dramatically impacted my life. As I've already confessed, I was an ultra-sensitive kid and loved all animals. I was also a privileged suburban kid and as such was ignorantly oblivious to the connection between animals (whom I loved) and my dinner plate. So, when I saw the bumper sticker

"Be Kind to Animals, Don't Eat Them"

(on some hippie van, obviously) I was more than a bit perplexed. That led me to read Peter Singer's philosophical treatise, "Animal Liberation," shortly thereafter making the announcement to my terribly disappointed parents that I was heretofore abstaining from eating, wearing, or using any products derived from the suffering of non-human animals.

And of course,
if they didn't do the same,
they were bigoted "speciesists."

Truly, is anything worse than a teenage evangelical, regardless of what philosophy they're shucking?

Having been enlightened from the tail-end of that VW Transporter, I followed suit years later on my first car, a bitchin' 1980 Camaro, by decorating it with a plethora of bumpers stickers, including the one that set me upon the path, "Be Kind to Animals, Don't Eat Them." For good measure, I also added, "Don't Have a Cow, Man" and of course, "Meat is Murder," which covered both my dietary ethics AND my musical preference for The Smiths. (No wonder I was such a depressive youngster.)

Right-Doing & Wrong-Doing

Nowadays, because everything is political, or so I am told, I'm seeing more bumper stickers than ever informing us how we *should* feel, what is right and even more so, what we should find viscerally wrong.

At a stoplight the other day I saw two cars side by side going at it politically via their bumper stickers:

The first car had a rainbow flag that read,

"Love is Love – I support Gay Marriage."

The second car sported one declaring,

"Holy Matrimony is between one man and one woman."

Honestly, I couldn't care less where each of these drivers stood on the issue of marriage; but at least their respective opinions seemed clear-cut.

However, there are often bumper stickers that are anything but clear, and below is a prime example:

If you're not angry, you're not paying attention

To what issue is this driver/wanna-be guru pointing?

Are they angry about high levels of illegal immigration
or about a proposed wall to prevent it?

Do they believe there are too many guns readily available
or are they pissed about some groups attempting to curb access to them?

Let's examine some potentially sketchy premises in play here:

1) If I am not focused and paying attention to the same specific situations and circumstances as this person, does that mean I'm not paying attention *generally*?
2) There is only one truly valid emotional response to those circumstances (anger).
3) Our emotional responses (feelings) can be directly caused by external circumstances; we are emotional victims of the world around us.

I have not found any of these to be true in my experience.

Even if I did believe premise number three to be valid, that feelings are caused by external circumstances, I could be focused on other things, such as the online video I saw of a police officer hugging and comforting a child with autism or a group of people saving a beached whale, the blooming of an orchid or even a field full of dandelions.

From these focal points I could create an equally true bumper sticker:

If you're not totally in awe of the beauty, love and kindness in the world, you're not paying attention.

People pay attention to different things at different times. Most people will give attention to those issues that *directly* affect them; not sure there's much to do about that, other than maybe a meta-level sharing of compassion, perhaps with the hope of a tipping point. I'm down with that.

To better understand both myself and others, my primary interest is to have a look at the premises and presuppositions people take to be true, often without much thought or investigation. In the case of the sentiment expressed on the bumper sticker in question—*if you're not angry, you're not paying attention*—if the driver believed the three premises above to be true (which I'm guessing most people do) then it makes fine sense to judge other people regarding:

1) what they are paying attention to and/ or presumably ignoring,

and

2) the emotions they either have or don't have about the particular situation.

I firmly believed all three of these premises for most of my young adult life—that is to say, that external circumstances caused my feelings, and that everyone should care about and feel the same as I did about all things.

As I look back on the actions I took based on my beliefs—many of them radically political in nature, what today might well be declared "domestic terrorism"—I don't feel that, overall, they were beneficial for me, to others, or to the world I was supposedly trying to make better. I was young and dumb and full of... righteous indignation. I was so damn sure I saw the truth, the whole truth and nothing but the truth, so help you God if you believed otherwise.

I'm not suggesting this is the sentiment of everyone who decorates their jalopies with bumper stickers. And to be clear, I'm not suggesting that anyone should or shouldn't be angry... or grateful, for that matter. I'm more curious about those people who are judging others for not experiencing the same emotions about the same issues.

It seems to me now that, no matter how insane it may look to me or others, people generally act in relatively rational ways, given the premises they take to be true at the moment,

and it is these *unexamined* premises
that erode the foundation for peace
and understanding
between
all people,
animals
and the planet.

Ponder-ables:

Pick a current personal belief, the stronger
the better—what are the foundational
premises upon which that belief rests?

What if those premises were a bit more
contextually pliable?

If you were to meet a diverse group of
people out in the field (the one beyond the
ideas of right and wrong), what might be
left to share and chat about?

CHAPTER TEN:
HOW TO MAKE LOVE STAY

"In the end we discover that to love and let go can be the same thing."
—*Jack Kornfield*

L-O-V-E

What a beautifully complex word/concept/feeling.

What does it evoke for you, in this moment?

Is it a warm and fuzzy sensation or maybe a trigger word?

For some people,
at least some of the time,
it can bring us together,
unite us,
and other times
it can seem almost as divisive as
God, Sex, Socialism,
or the band Nickelback.

Most of us think of love in relation to our feelings towards another human being, *within relationship*, and that is the context of love for this essay. However, I'm going to take a bit of an abstract approach to the topic, and how to make it stay.

Abstraction, really, you don't say?

Indeed, because more often than not, I find it beneficial to explore from the UNIVERSAL perspective, what is Capitol T-True for everyone and everything before pondering the more specific, personal situation or question at hand. The universal perspective often feels more abstract, at least initially, but also assists us in setting the stage prior to looking at the more personal aspects.

That is why I'm inclined to start abstractly universal, regardless of the specific topic. I'm hoping at least some of you can appreciate, or at least tolerate this approach. I have plenty of feedback that it can be frustrating at times and that I'm an acquired taste, that it may or may not be worth the effort.

Side Note (1): I purchased a T-shirt while on the Bourbon Trail:

I'd rather be someone's shot of whiskey than everyone's cup of tea.

Still with me? Swell.

If we look at love as a positive mental/emotional state just like joy, happiness, and peace of mind—trying to figure out how to make it stay presupposes at least four things:

1) love is something that exists outside of us
2) love can be acquired and subsequently lost
3) there is a method(s) to keeping love captive and
4) it would be a good idea to employ one or more of these methods

If we take all four of these presuppositions to be true (consciously or otherwise), it would make perfect sense to discover the methods for making love stay and utilize them.

After all, if we value love, and we are always at risk of losing it... well, desperate times call for desperate measures.

For guidance in this regard, I suggest we turn to writer, poet, guru and, I'll admit it, my artist man-crush, Tom Robbins, from his first (and in my opinion, finest work) *Still Life With Woodpecker*:

Who knows how to make love stay?

1. Tell love you are going to Junior's Deli on Flatbush Avenue in Brooklyn to pick up a cheesecake, and if love stays, it can have half. It will stay.

2. Tell love you want a memento of it and obtain a lock of its hair. Burn the hair in a dime-store incense burner with yin/yang symbols on three sides. Face southwest. Talk fast over the burning hair in a convincingly exotic language. Remove the ashes of the burnt hair and use them to paint a mustache on your face. Find love. Tell it you are someone new. It will stay.

3. Wake love up in the middle of the night. Tell it the world is on fire. Dash to the bedroom window and pee out of it. Casually return to bed and assure love that everything is going to be all right. Fall asleep. Love will be there in the morning.

Side Note (2a): My brother recited the above passage as a reading at our wedding (my wife is a saint for putting up with my eccentricities).

Side Note (2b): At least once a month I perform the third ritual; not so much in an attempt to make love stay, but more because it's super fun, at least for guys, or maybe just for me, to pee out of windows.

I had always believed that what Tom was suggesting with his satirical slant on these three tactics, and that was finally confirmed the last time in conversation with him over drinks in Los Angeles (which never really happened, obviously), is the fact that ANY type of action taken in an attempt to make love stay is rather absurd, and founded upon popular misunderstandings of the origin of love, and how it and all other feelings (good and other-than-good) actually work.

In other words, words not so obnoxiously long-winded... you ARE love. It does not reside outside of you, and that is why your quest for it will always end in vain, at least until you turn INWARD. You (and me, and most everybody at one time or another) have fallen for the illusion of an external origin of love; and so, we are like a dog chasing its own tail, always sensing it is
so close
and
yet
so elusive.

Seeking advice on how to make love stay would be akin to the dog looking for advice on how to be more stealthy in its tail-catching skills. That dog can become a Canine Ninja and still never succeed in catching its tail. Of course, he doesn't have to catch it, it's already part of him. Can you imagine the sense of relief, not to mention the savings in time, energy, and frustration this pup could feel when this understanding finally reveals itself to him?

"Looking for love" and "trying to make love stay" are equally fruitless endeavors, because we are always looking in the wrong places. We are attempting to imprison something already built within the very foundation of our souls. Such a misguided quest only feeds an unnecessary sense of existential angst.

If we are the essence of love itself, which I sense to be True, then why isn't it more obvious, why can't we see it? Within Eastern spiritual traditions, there is a popular analogy about veils which impede our vision. In other words, we have perfect vision, but our ability to clearly see and access this innate knowing is clouded by veils of multiple origins, i.e., cultural conditioning, beliefs, fear, etc.

Again, I will default to Rumi:

"Your task is not to seek for love, but merely to seek and find all the barriers within yourself that you have built against it."

Rumi isn't suggesting we do anything, aside from finding and identifying the barriers (veils) that separate us from the recognition of our inherent nature as love itself. Once the Truth is seen, the process of Awakening is initiated.

Ponder-ables:

How have you hunted for love? How have you attempted to imprison it?

What veils have you built up, consciously or otherwise, that may be obscuring your recognition of the love within and all around you?

CHAPTER ELEVEN: THE PEOPLE NEVER/ALWAYS CHANGE PARADOX

"The best thing about a picture is that it never changes, even when the people in it do."

—Andy Warhol

The focal point of this essay is the humdinger of a paradox—people *never* change and simultaneously, people *always* change.

Do People Change?

That is the question.

Answer: Of course they do... and of course they don't.

That is to say, in my incomprehensibly incomplete understanding, the Capital-T Truth of our Being *never* changes, it is formless and foundational, after all. On the other foot, all the attributes within the world of form, including our personal psychologies we hold so dear, those are about as permanent as the steam coming off a dog turd in the snow.

As Alan Watts may have quipped, "You're under no obligation to be the same person you were five minutes ago." I would go so far as to add you couldn't even if you tried.

My Love/Hate Relationship with Change

Most of my coaching clients initially engage with me because they want to change something; maybe they want to "lose" a particular behavior or "gain" a sense of meaning or purpose in their lives.

But ultimately, they want to change how they FEEL.

Years ago, I was rather proficient (relatively speaking) at playing The Change Game. I even considered myself a "change worker" and was into both mental/emotional state manipulation and behavioral modification.

Change is a major focus in the self-improvement world. However, there are several assumptions at play here that deserve a bit of scrutiny:

1) There exists a "self" (one that is separate)

2) This self is in need of improvement

3) There is a standard against which this self is to be judged

4) You, or perhaps you and a teacher/ psychologist/guru are the best option to lead this improvement mission

Yeah, I'm calling bullshit.

At best, it's a well-intended lie.

I am suggesting WHO YOU ARE never changes (and therefore cannot be improved upon), but the costumes you wear and the roles you play in the drama within the external world are in constant flux.

So, what *exactly* are we trying to improve upon with these changes?

The popular image is always climbing upwards—a ladder, or staircase, maybe even an elevator if you spend enough money to get the fancy metaphors.

However, what if all the *real* stuff, the nitty-gritty foundational Truth, is at the ground level, within the foundation itself? What if instead of striving, climbing, scaling and clawing our way upwards towards the distant outreaches with our obsession for ascension, we instead honored our roots, sat down, maybe even laid our asses down, and rested within our *home base*?

Insecurity & Instantaneous Change

George and Linda Pransky are 3P-based psychologists and pioneers in introducing this perspective to mainstream practitioners worldwide. I hold *The Relationship Handbook* in the highest regard and the best resource for all things "relational" (see *Resources for Further Exploration*).

The Pranskys consider *insecurity* to be the prominent, generic mental illness at large today and the origin of all maladaptive behavior. As a person begins to CTFD, their insecurities naturally lessen, and they return to a state of their True Nature, their Home Base.

So, it's a sort of a change, sure, but it's even more of a *return*. It's not an improvement, except in the sense of how good it always feels to be back home when you've been away for a long time.

Without insecurity muddying up our mental waters, change is often effortless and instantaneous.

As a matter of fact, I am going to suggest that change most often occurs in exactly this way: effortlessly and instantaneously. It just doesn't always feel that way.

And what of the popular notion that because you've *"been this way for so long, it will take a long time to change"*?

Consider this:

You've been wearing a pair of shoes for the last several years that no longer fit properly; they are three sizes too small. Not only that, you've been unknowingly wearing them on the wrong feet.

Your feet don't feel great,
but you've gotten used to it.
It's just the way your feet feel.
(Read: "It's just the way I am.")

Then someone is kind enough to point out that your shoes seem a bit small, and perhaps even on the other-than-proper feet.

You might initially feel a bit embarrassed, but eventually you would feel relieved and thankful for the insight.

How long would it take you to get a properly fitted pair of shoes, and to ensure you wear them on the correct feet?

Are you with me here?

Your behavior would change instantaneously with your new understanding of the optimal way shoes worked.

Sure, you might, out of habit, grab your old pair sometimes; but when you put those Chinese-foot-binding-inspired kicks on, you would no doubt quickly realize/remember that you know a different way now: a way more fitting, more natural and more true to you.

The Bottom Line

The real, true and formless you never changes.

Everything within the world of form is in a constant state of change.

We do have an element of influence in regard to how things change, but it is not to be found in the ever-popular domain of control or through effort and force.

The best way to elicit allow change is to set up the ideal environment for it. That means to let go of struggle, and instead connect with your innate sense of well-being. When you have a high level of internal security, your counterproductive behaviors will rarely even occur to you.

But please don't take my word for it, just...

Notice
CTFD
Do Nothing

and watch the change
roll in ecstasy at your feet.
(apologies to Franz Kafka)

Ponder-ables:

What if (meaningful) change was always effortless and instantaneous?

How would you spend all the extra time (and effort) you would save by not working so hard to be better?

What if it's all just been a misunderstanding about the best way to walk in which shoes?

CHAPTER TWELVE:
THE TAO OF TEAM—
THE SCIENCE & ART OF
EFFORTLESS COLLABORATION

"The Gulf Stream will flow through a straw provided the straw is aligned to the Gulf Stream, and not at cross purposes with it."
—Anne Lamott, Bird by Bird

It may come as a mild surprise, or perhaps even a bit of a shock/horror, to learn that I occasionally present "team building" seminars to major corporations. I hardly own a decent dress shirt, not a single tie, and my overall "vibe" couldn't be less corporate.

However, this oddity of a situation has come to pass as several private clients experienced their own insights from taking a gander in the direction of an inside-out and non-dual perspective and believed what they discovered would be useful to their teams.

And they're right, of course.

Understanding how

your mind works,
the origin of your
internal experiences,
and who you really are
elevates *everything* and
every aspect of your life,
including the workplace.

I'll share some of the exploratory highlights from corporate team seminars on how these perspectives ultimately produce better outcomes. These shifts in productivity were accompanied by a lowering of previewed stress levels and elevated enjoyment and job satisfaction.

You may find these highlights useful, whether you are part of a team at work or otherwise, because a relationship is a relationship, regardless of titles and specific circumstances. Keep in mind that your "team" need not only be your fellow sales associates at work, but can include your sports teammates, condo association members, and of course, your family (bloodline or chosen).

Note: Many of the overall concepts presented in this chapter are from an excellent book on utilizing a Three Principles Perspective in a corporate environment titled *Invisible Power* by Ken Manning, Robin Charbit, and Sandra Krot. (See *Resources for Further Exploration*.)

The Foundational Importance of State of Mind

All problems are, at their core, state of mind problems.

And the only "problem" is a simple mis-understanding.

I've grown hesitant to use the phrase "state of mind" or "mindset" in corporate training seminars, as it is prone to elicit audible groans from the peanut gallery. But I get it. I mean, how many more times can people hear some hyper-caffeinated motivational coach spouting off about the importance of mindset, right? That is so 2015.

So, a couple pieces of good news to put you at ease:

1) I'm not a normal coach (corporate or otherwise)
2) There will be no techniques or exercises designed to train your brain for "The Ultimate Mindset"

As a reminder, this perspective is descriptive, not prescriptive. We won't be dealing with applications, but rather reaping the benefits of the implications gained from this new perspective and understanding.

I won't be sharing tips and tricks because

there's nothing you must DO in order to benefit and fully optimize your mind. As a matter of fact, I will continually suggest that you DO LESS,

perhaps less
than even
seems responsible.

I'm not the least bit interested
in the feelings of being responsible,
I'm interested in your RESULTS.

But more than that
I'm interested in
how you feel
in the process
of getting there.

The Essay Title Breakdown

So, what's up with the fancy hodge-podge title of this essay?

We've got Taoism, Science, Art and Collaboration.

Let's take these bird by bird...

Taoism

Taoism is a spiritual, philosophical, religious paradigm from Ancient China. It's founder, Lao Tzu, was a contemporary of Confucius, who is more well known in the West, primarily because of cookies (Confucius say....). Lao Tzu and Confucius had quite differing styles and *modi operandi*. Confucius dictated the exact behaviors for how to be an upstanding Chinese citizen; there were proper ways to sit, stand, eat, even for dropping the kids off at the pool. Lao Tzu, on the other foot, was more of a go-with-the-flow type of guy, something like The Dude from *The Big Lebowski*.

The Tao can be translated as "the Way." One of the more telling elements of this philosophy is, "The Tao that can be spoken of isn't the Tao."

Can you already smell the similarity between The Tao and The Inside-Out Understanding? Both are purely descriptive. Neither speaks to the limited depth of understanding available from the intellectual side of the equation. Both perspectives deepen as we continue to explore and allow our embodied wisdom of their inherent Truth to come forth.

If you'd like to find out more about Taoism, certainly check out the original text, *The Tao Te Ching*—it's a beautiful little book—and my personal favorite, *The Tao of Pooh*. (Just to be clear, that's P-o-o-h, as in the bear, not p-o-o, like a bowel movement.)

The Science

Although my favorite scientific discoveries are in the more recent "quantum physics" arena, there are some rather neat-o findings dating back to the fifties. There is a decent level of agreement among scientists (which is about the best you'll ever get) about how it is that we humans process information from the outside world and "make sense" of it.

Those in the world of Neuro-Linguistic Programming (NLP) describe the filtering process of the vast amount of information we take in (some estimates are upwards of 11 million bits per second) as consisting mainly of Generalization, Deletion, and Distortion. These are not negative processes. As a matter of fact, they are crucial to our being able to function within Relative Reality.

What is vital to keep in mind, is that none of us process outside information in exactly the same way. Furthermore, we are all only making our "best guess" as to what is outside of us. A prime example of this is when you see your friend walking towards you from three blocks away. You start waving and shouting their name, only to realize as they get closer that (much to your horrific embarrassment) it wasn't your friend after all.

We are always "guessing" and are never truly 100% accurate in any objective sense.

No two people will have the exact same read on "reality." We are all living in our own thought-generated individual reality, being created moment to moment. It's NOT just different perceptions. It's not that we see the same thing differently, it's that we actually see different things. That's just the way it is, and it doesn't have to be a problem. It can be exciting, productive and the source of infinite potential. It's only problematic when we don't understand how our minds work (from the inside-out), and we are constantly in battle with other people to defend our own thought-created reality in this moment.

The Art

This is where the fun part truly begins.

The primary question being,

"What kind of cool shit do we want to create?"

Collaboration

There are two essential elements that reliably foster effective collaboration among humans:

1) *Clarity of Mind*
Once we understand how minds work, where our experience of life originates, and remember who/what we are, something invariably happens— our minds settle and we Calm The Fuck Down.
When it comes to creative problem-solving, it is immensely helpful to have a settled mind, one with space for insights to emerge.

Note: This is always an endeavor of *subtraction*, not addition.

2) *Communication*
Once individuals on a team have clarity of mind, communication tends to be free-flowing and relatively risk-free, both critical components for healthy dialog and brainstorming.

It can be that simple. And that is good news, considering "Communication Skills Training" gets an even less enthusiastic reception than "Mindset Training" from most seminar attendees.

This is not to imply that exercises like staring into a co-worker's eyes for ten minutes, or classification systems like the DISC profiles, or studying the techniques of Nonviolent Communication (NVC) are without merit. It's just that I personally love that stuff about as much as a thumbtack in my taint. And I wouldn't dare suggest you do things that I personally eschew at all costs.

Additionally, without an embodied understanding of the source of our experience, it can be challenging to call upon the tools learned from these systems when you need them the most. With a deep understanding, you can often mess up the verbiage and delivery and still be seen and heard authentically.

Once you come to understand how *your* mind works, you will understand how *all* minds work, and that alone will impact your relations with your teammates, family and elsewhere. Then you can layer on those other techniques and strategies much more effectively, as much as seems appropriate and useful.

Difficult People

"Trying to understand some people is like trying to smell the color 9."

Everyone is psychologically innocent, including you.

That "difficult" person isn't difficult, they are simply acting in accordance with their current-moment thinking. If you were to have the same thinking in that moment, and took it to be real, you would likely act the same way.

This happens in life and in the workplace *all the time.* A coworker will be stressed and acting like a maniac not realizing it's simply the quality of their thinking in the moment. This lack of awareness often feeds into a sense of self-righteousness about the situation and buying into the illusion that current circumstances have created their current feelings.

Often, YOU are part of those said current circumstances.

Instead of being defensive and reacting to their state, further perpetuating the misunderstanding, you can recognize they are simply caught up in their own thinking and acting from that state of mind.

And because we all know quite well how easy it is to fall for the illusion, this creates the insight and natural arising of EMPATHY. It's hard to be a human sometimes.

Team Synergy

It seems to me there are two critical elements that birth and support synergy among teams of any sort.

1) *CTFD:* The ability to recognize when we are caught up in our thinking, and simply allow the mind to settle. The beauty of

being part of a team is it takes only one person to come to their (natural) senses and begin the positive trajectory towards unity and productivity.

2) *Curiosity:* When team members understand and respect that each person is creating and living within their own separate reality, moment to moment, they can look for the wisdom each individual can contribute.

"You are always more alike other people than you are different. Your humanity precedes your personality or momentary perspective. As you understand more and more about how the mind works, you catch yourself putting up artificial barriers between yourself and other people." —Ken Manning, Invisible Power

Ponder-ables:

What if that "difficult" co-worker really wasn't?

What if differences in perspectives were celebrated; as in asking, "Really, tell me more about how that looks to you?"

What if empathy was our default response to teammates behaving other-than-we-would-prefer?

CHAPTER THIRTEEN: THE LIFE (AND DEATH) LESSONS OF YOUTH SPORTS

"I do not like sports, unless you consider treating all humankind with love and respect a sport."

—Todd Barry

Youth sports can provide a plethora of life lessons for kids and teenagers. In this essay, let's explore the obvious positive and perhaps more subtle and potentially detrimental components of the curriculum.

I am aware the "and Death" portion of this title may seem a bit extremist, but I'm not talking about literal physical death. Instead, I'm pointing towards the potential damage to the human spirit; specifically, the mental /emotional well-being of youngsters participating in athletic competitions.

I recently consulted with the mother of a 13-year-old regarding excessive anxiety around her golf performance. What might be the true origins of these common feelings of anxiety around playing a game?

Side Note: Although we'll be addressing this

with an athletic example, it applies equally to any form of competition among young people, from the arts to academics and everything in between.

Before we dive in, full disclosure: I don't have any biological children, at least to the best of my knowledge. I did make money hand over fist to subsidize my graduate school studies with donations to a San Francisco sperm bank, so who knows.

However, I have had the privilege of coaching over a hundred junior athletes over the past 24 years. I feel as though this has given me a rather unique perspective on how young people view themselves in general, and in relationship to their chosen athletic endeavors specifically. My experience is both from a position once removed, yet often with an insider's view that parents aren't privy to; these kids will often tell me about feelings they're not willing or able to fully express to their parents.

The Good Lessons

It is a common and relatively accepted belief that sports teach children life lessons. Fair enough. Some of the most common lessons that are said to be cultivated via youth sports are:

Work Ethic

Leadership
Dedication
Commitment
Optimism
Confidence
Teamwork
Sportsmanship

I trust we can all agree these are solid virtues, and if these are the lessons being taught and acquired, then bravo. Perhaps those are the ideal and intended lessons; however, the real test of any learning environment should probably be measured by how many students seem to fully integrate those intended lessons as opposed to less-optimal, self-limiting beliefs about the origin of their own self-worth.

The Other-Than-Good Potential (and Untrue) Lessons

Below is a partial conversation I had with a golf coach that may shed some light on my current perspective.

I was approached by the coach of a competitive high school golf team, one that routinely is in contention for the state championship each year. She asked me to work with her golfers on reducing their anxiety before tournaments. It was obvious to me that she was a committed and caring coach, as she had already worked with numerous licensed PhD sports psychologists. She had introduced her players to various forms of stress reduction with breathing, heart rate, hypnosis, meditation, you name it. She was hoping (with the best of intentions) for yet another trick, tool or technique for her players to employ to quell their pre-round anxiety.

She looked a bit surprised and perplexed when I told her it sounded like their mental game toolbox was plenty full already, maybe even overflowing.

She inquired, "Well, if you wouldn't teach them something to do, how would you help them not feel anxious before a round?"

I told her that I'd be most interested in WHY they were feeling anxious.

She replied, in a way that implied it should be acutely obvious, "Because they might not play well, and they might lose."

I responded, "Well, that's always a possibility. But why would that possibility drive thought patterns that in turn create anxious feelings?"

She gave me this look, the kind of look a dog gives you where they cock their head to one side—it's a look I get a lot, actually, so I continued.

"It's been my experience that most kids, at a fundamental level, get caught in these anxious thought cycles about performance because they have a fundamental misunderstanding: that there is something *real* at risk. And by real, I mean pretty much the only *REAL thing—who and what they are.* They have come to equate their current and upcoming performance with their Innate OK-ness. And when someone (of any age) believes this to be true (even subconsciously), of course it feeds into anxiety.

In Truth, they're already and always OK, how they perform can't touch that. When they know that, at the deepest level, their anxiety will dissipate."

The coach nodded and then asked, "How do we teach my players THAT?"

"That, I said, cannot be taught, at least in any meaningful way. Rather, it is shown and shared through all interactions and attitudes towards them in and around their performances, as well as elsewhere.

I asked her, "Do you react differently to your players when they do exceptionally well as compared to playing poorly?"

She said, "I try to respond enthusiastically to good play and in an empathetic way to someone having a bad round."

I told her, "I'm sure you do, and that sounds both appropriate and compassionate. How about the parents?"

She went silent and a cringing, slightly painful expression made its way across her face. "They all mean well and want the best for their kids, but they seem to have a lot riding on their child's performance. What would you suggest?"

I replied, "I would suggest, not that it would be easy, but to act *exactly* the same after a round where their daughter shoots 68 or 86. Perhaps saying something along the lines of,

'I love
to watch
you play.'

And then go and get ice cream or whatever the usual post tournament ritual might be."

"Wow, she said, I'm not sure how they're going to respond to that suggestion. Of course, they're excited when their daughter shoots low but disappointed, for her, when she blows up."

"Sure, that's understandable. But keep in mind, these kids are picking up signals, both consciously and unconsciously, ALL THE TIME. When they experience the elation of their parents when they play well, and then just the quiet reservation when they play poorly, that is a *sharp contrast*, and can be interpreted as how the parents and others feel about them, and that the variance is dependent upon their performance. I'm not suggesting it's true, that they actually feel like their kids are not as worthy when they play poorly, not at all, but we're talking about how it may *feel* to the *kid*; what lesson she may be inadvertently learning."

This is an example of "going upstream" with the issue of pre-performance anxiety. Instead of teaching a new technique to quiet it down for the moment, we look to show them their foundational grounded-ness.

Do they know they are OK, no matter what; no matter how they perform?

For the Love of the Game

How easy it is to forget (for kids and adults alike) that it's just a game and games are to be played for the LOVE of the game itself.

I'll often ask a parent if their kid *loves* the game of golf. They always respond YES. And then I follow up with, "Or do they just love winning?" Being competitive and having a strong desire to win is part of what makes games fun, but if you truly love your sport, you love it *regardless of* if you win or lose.

And that is possible
when you fully understand
that winning or losing
doesn't mean a damn thing
about you,
your opponent
or the game.

If a young golfer loves the game, and has an inherent understanding of her own, untouchable OK-ness, then she will be thrilled for the opportunity to be on the 18th green with a double-breaker 20-footer to win the state championship. She will be excited, but not pressured, because this is what the game is all about—playing—and there's no pressure because it's ONLY a state title on the line, not her value as a beautiful human spirit.

There are indeed plenty of valuable lessons that can be learned from youth sports. But my hope, and some will say that I'm a dreamer, is that as our kids, and they're **all our kids**, wake up to their True Nature, and bring that lesson onto the playing fields of all sports, and the game of life, and positively impact everyone that they encounter, both teammates and opponents.

Ponder-ables:

What if in the past when you felt anxious about some aspect of performance, it wasn't about your performance, but about your innate self-worth?

The line between anxiety and excitement is quite thin. Can you sense that the feelings you were labeling as anxiety might easily shift to excitement with an understanding that you were already and always OK, no matter the outcome of this event?

What could be more valuable, more affirming, for the children of the world, than the gift of insight into their undeniable goodness, than the freedom to play all-out, because there is nothing real at risk?

Reminder: YOU are a child of this world, too.

BREATHE

CHAPTER FOURTEEN:
STAND YOUR GROUND

The tallest tree in the forest was once just a little nut that held its ground.

If you will allow me a modest indulgence, I'd like to piggyback off the last essay and share a snapshot from my personal teen-angst sports saga/drama history books.

I was fifteen years old when I started "acting out." My transformation was considered "extreme" by my rather traditional suburbanite parents and peers, even though the alternative choices and changes I was adopting were limited to my physical appearance, diet, and participation in sports. I dyed my hair platinum blond and spiked it straight up, got five piercings, wore eyeliner, and dressed like Johnny Rotten of The Sex Pistols.

This was rather shocking for a "fly-over state" in 1984.

I had unknowingly become a Straight Edger, as that trend hadn't yet hit my part of the country. For me it just meant no drugs or alcohol, no use of animal products for food or clothing, and an appreciation for hardcore punk music. I would never have bought into the SE philosophy regarding abstinence from sexual relations, though.

That would have been silly.

Although I may have looked like trouble, I created almost none. I got good (enough) grades and was quite frankly, a damn decent kid.

Then I did
the unthinkable:
I quit
playing
football
(quarterback, no less).

Looking like a punk-ass freak was one thing, but quitting football was a profane act of defiance against all that was good and holy. After all, high school football was a sacred cow, and I had the audacity to kill it.

The head football coach pulled me out of a math class (midway through an exam, mind you), sat me down in his office and asked me,

"Have you lost your Goddamn mind?"

And so it began.

As it turns out, I hadn't lost my mind. However, I also hadn't anticipated just how much loss was headed my way: reputation, social status, sense of self, and most of my friendships.

I was deeply lonely for the first time in my life. And I was bitter.

By outward appearances, everything about me screamed, "I don't give a fuck what you think!" while on the inside all I craved, from the depth of my teenage soul, was to be loved and accepted.

I see it so clearly now; I was testing everyone all the time.
How dare you judge me by my hairstyle or because I don't drink beer!

If I don't look like Bobby and Tommy, you won't like me anymore?

Really?

If I don't play the same game (literally), you won't accept me?

Is this friendship?
Is this love?

Of course, it wasn't their fault, no one likes to be tested. And they were all just longing to belong as well.

And my parents just wanted to save me the suffering of "not fitting in" that was part and parcel of being at all different from your peers during that stage of life.

And that head coach, he was just doing what made sense to him to do at the time.

There was no ill-intent and therefore no fault to go around.

As I mentioned in the previous essay, I've had the privilege to work with dozens of junior athletes over the last three decades. My position as a trusted coach, combined with my non-parental persona (I'm older than their parents, but *seem* so different—tattoos, piercings, and all), allows them to share many of their personal struggles with me.

It is heart-breaking at times, but ultimately heart-warming.

Stand Your Ground

As I trust you know by now, I'd rather get a reach-around from Edward Scissorhands than give anyone advice. That being said, here is my completely unsolicited and grain-of-salt observation/suggestion:

The more a kid acts like they don't give a fuck, the MORE they care.

And the most impactful action one can take as a parent, teacher, coach, or a friend is to *stand your ground in love and compassion.*

No matter what they throw at you, batten down your own emotional hatches, weather the storm, stand your ground and tell (better yet *show*) them that you love them for who they really are, not their latest fashion choices (no matter how awful), not their current phase of musical appreciation (even if it truly is "just noise") and not for how they choose to express themselves as they grow into and own the beauty of self-discovery.

We all seek love and acceptance,
especially those who shun it.

We all deserve love and acceptance,
especially those who appear to run from it.

Please,
stand
your
ground.

Ponder-ables:

How can we stand our ground in love and compassion for those we care about, especially when they act in ways counter to our preferences?

How might we consciously expand that circle to include "others," strangers, even those we perceive as opponents in whatever capacity?

And finally—and this may be a bit of crazy-talk—but can we include ourselves in this circle?

SECTION iii: (no) SELF-IMPROVEMENT PROTOCOLS

CHAPTER FIFTEEN:
THE ORIGIN STORY FETISH

"It's no use going back to yesterday, because I was a different person then."
—Alice, in Wonderland

In this essay we'll ponder upon the utility (or lack thereof) of what I call "deep past origin stories," and the fetish-like preoccupation with identifying the historical origin of WHY we behave in certain ways, have peculiar personality traits, tendencies, fears etc.

I'm not dissing on fetishes, origin story-based or otherwise, as I've got a couple of dozen at last count. However, I find it useful and sometimes illuminating to peek under the hood and ascertain the utility of each fetish, and if the payoff of maintaining it is worthwhile.

As a toddler I was quite annoying for many reasons (or so I am told), one of which being my incessant asking of "Why?" about everything and of everyone. Apparently, it was one of my first words and far and away my favorite. That didn't change much as I matured, and my high school teachers and college professors seemed equally as annoyed as my family members much of the time.

My personal journey centered around the usual Big Why inquiries; specifically, why did I have certain behavioral tendencies and beliefs that held me back, and why did other people have their own. This led to an exploratory journey into my upbringing, my parents, early impactful experiences (some while still just a bun in the oven), and even... I'll admit it, from potential past lives.

All these avenues were intellectually and often emotionally stimulating. Not always fun, but rarely boring. As different as some of these psychological practices and theories were, they consistently had two things in common:

1) They were all focused on the past
2) They were all modestly helpful, at best, in the long run

Perhaps like you, I've spent a couple hundred hours (and over $15,000) on various therapies—from the Freudian to the Freakish (and certainly the freakish parts of the Freudian model).

I honestly don't regret any of it... what would be the point? Who knows how paths merge and diverge, and we eventually end up exactly where we belong?

Hell, can it be otherwise?

My experiences with psychological therapies are the reason I chose *not* to pursue a graduate degree in that field, and instead embarked on the much less reasonable major track of Eastern Philosophy & Religion. As I would come to find out, the job prospects for such majors are limited to further ivory tower academia or managing a Waffle House (both equally unattractive options for me at that time; however, it did allow me the opportunity to discover The Waffle House Secret Menu Item #154).

Coaching vs. Psychotherapy

There is an important distinction between therapy and coaching, legally in most states and ethically in my mind and coaching practice. To keep this simple (meaning it will certainly be oversimplified), therapy deals with a diagnosis of conditions and seeks to heal a dysfunction. Transformative Coaching, at least in the way that I practice it, presupposes that every person already possesses innate well-being.

No one is broken
and therefore no one
needs to be "cured"
of any dysfunction.

This might be an apropos time to explain what I mean by Transformative Life Coaching, and how it may differ from other types of coaching. The difference between a more traditional Life Coach and a Transformative Coach is that the former is helpful/useful/a problem solver—i.e., weight loss, job/life transition, public speaking etc.

A Transformative Coach provides the space and conditions for transforming a client's relationship to life and to whatever the "problem" might be. "Trans" means to change the relationship to the issue (form itself), i.e., *how* you relate to your weight, your job, speaking in public or whatever.

Michael Neill puts forth three main aims of Transformative Coaching in his excellent book, *Super Coach*:

1) *Wake Up:* To provide the conditions by which a client is more easily able to wake up FROM the dream, the illusion of the outside/in paradigm and to the infinite potential of life that is to be had with the Inside-Out understanding.

2) *Move beyond One's Personal Psychology:* That is to say, stop focusing on our personalities, our individual hang-ups, our stories. Of course, we still have them, I have mine and you have yours. It's just that our true freedom isn't to be found, or retrieved, by working on them, but rather by recognizing their limited value.

3) *Create Cool Shit:* As one wakes up and moves beyond a personal psychology, true freedom can be experienced, and creativity often flows forth from that liberated state. Cool shit can vary greatly from human to human, which is most excellent. Once you have reclaimed your freedom, what you do with it, where you direct your passions, what you choose to create, that's up to you, and none of my business. Go forth and prosper.

Origin Stories, Past and Present

Many of my coaching clients have a history with traditional therapy or psychoanalysis. When searching for "the why" of a long-suffered feeling state, such therapies will often look for an origin story; the event(s) which shaped and molded your personal psychology and world view. The idea is that an understanding of the past origin story will free you from its grip and minimize or eliminate the effects in the present.

It's not as though this process *never* works. There are plenty of people for whom it seems to have been of great benefit. It's just that the overall success rates seem quite low. And even when it does work, it often takes a *long* time, can be emotionally painful, and dreadfully expensive.

As
always,
there
is another
way.

Instead of digging through the archives of your past in search of an ancient origin story, I'm personally more interested in *the present moment origin story*.

At first glance that may seem a bit off; how can the present moment have a present moment origin story? However, when we consider that THOUGHT is ever present and always creating our moment-to-moment internal interpretation of the external world, it follows that thought itself is always the origin of whatever we are feeling in the present moment.

But for present moment thought, including the thought of a past event, could you possibly have a present moment feeling? Could you possibly have a story without thought in the present moment?

I'm certainly not suggesting that things in the past didn't occur, perhaps some shitty things happened, and hopefully some blissful experiences as well. What I am putting forth is that they're not happening NOW. And if they're part of your internal experience now, if you're having feelings about them, whether limiting or empowering in nature, *it is by way of thought.*

Thought
is always
the origin story
of the very next
feeling state...
moment to
moment to
moment to
moment.

As already stated, I'm not a fan of just doing "positive thinking" or any type of thought policing/manipulation. I find attempting to control my every thought as a means to manage my emotional state quite exhausting and nearly impossible in the long-term.

Instead, it is the insightful understanding that *thought is the precursor to feelings* that is ultimately liberating. There's no need to control your thoughts, they're nice sometimes and utterly bat-shit insane other times; but once you see their transient nature, that they come and go, just like the feelings they evoke, they lose any power over you. Or rather, you realize that they never had any power over you.

And you are only ever
one thought away

from a new origin story
and a fresh feeling state.

This means that if I'm feeling nervous in a new situation, it's not because of an embarrassing experience I suffered as a child when attempting a new endeavor; rather it's because I'm having "nervous thoughts" in the present moment, which is directly eliciting my current nervous feelings.

Keeping It Simple

As has already been established, I am a simple man. And to my simple mind, it makes more sense that my current feelings are shadows of my current thinking, as opposed to hypothetically being the result of experiences in the past. I'm not saying this is true, just that it looks that way to me. I don't have scientific proof, but anecdotally I do know when I THINK about my past experiences, they seem to affect me in the present, and when I'm not thinking about them, they do not.

The process of thinking is the constant, and the content of the thoughts is the variable that produces my feelings in the moment.

Is time all but an illusion? Does the past exist? These are questions well beyond my cranial capacity and pay-grade. But it sure looks to me like *all* parts of our individual and collective journeys should be honored, and that our past experiences do indeed play a role in shaping the heroes and heroines we are all destined to become.

That being said, ponder and explore for yourself the utility of effort in sorting through your past for particular events you've been told are the key to present day limiting beliefs and behaviors. Or perhaps, look to the more recent past, like seconds ago, and the origin story of that thought train, and where it's headed.

Thought is the paintbrush. Your consciousness is the canvas; your innate creative potential is the paint. You, of course, are the artist. There is an endless supply of blank canvases. Go ahead, darken the page.

Ponder-ables:

Do you personally find that exploring origin stories from your past, that supposedly affect your mental states and behavior in the present, is helpful in moving past these states and behaviors?

What if you weren't broken in any regard? What if there was nothing in your past you had to overcome?

CHAPTER SIXTEEN:
LET GO OR BE DRAGGED

*"When I let go of what I am,
I become what I might be.
When I let go of what I have,
I receive what I need."*

— Tao Te Ching

In case you have any doubts about it, water torture sucks. When inflicted by your so-called friends, that's some next level shit.

I was lured into said predicament under false pretenses—a fun day at the lake with food, girls in skimpy bathing suits, and water skiing. I enthusiastically agreed to attend, as all I heard and imagined were the cheerleaders from my high school in itsy bitsy teeny-weeny bikinis; I didn't catch the bit about water skiing.

Somehow, despite having grown up living less than a mile from a body of water, I never learned to water ski. Like any normal fifteen-year-old, I was insanely insecure and nervous about the potential of losing street cred among my peers.

For contextual purposes, you may recall that I was the quarterback for the football team. Like many socially conditioned teens, I equated my self-worth with this identity as an athlete and leader. Truth be told, though: it was a bit of a sham. You see, I was old for my grade with a late Virgo birthday, and I matured quite early (I was already shaving in eighth grade). I basically got a head-start in terms of physicality. I was bigger and stronger than other kids in my class. That was the predominant reason I excelled early in athletics, not because of an abundance of natural talent. I suppose I was an early adopter of Impostor Syndrome. This is all to set the scene that within the world of teen-angst, there was a lot at risk for me in this watery horror show scenario.

I Once Was Lost, But Now I am Found

I nervously suited up with my lifejacket, disembarked from the boat and plunged into the water.

I already didn't like this. Not one bit.

I was peppered with a barrage of newbie instructions by my well-intentioned and water-skiing proficient posse. Shortly thereafter, the boat accelerated, and I managed to follow all their cues and get upright. I was speeding along quite nicely on my very first run, thank you very much... until I wasn't.

I got a bit out over the skis, literally and figuratively, and took a nose-dive into the lake. Not a big deal, usually. However, there was a valuable piece of advice omitted during my instructional briefing—likely because they assumed it was self-evident—which was to...

Let go of the fucking rope when you fall.

Instead, I instinctively applied a death-grip, which almost led to my actual death, as I was dragged at high speeds through the waves. My so-called friends could have cut the engine right away but chose otherwise. I'm convinced it was intentional, to create humor at my expense.

While torpedoing through wake after wake, I'm sure that I swallowed half the lake, and perhaps an entire fish, which was quite traumatic for me, being a vegan and all.

I also lost my swimsuit,
which was traumatic
for everyone else.

Finally, after practically drudging the bottom of the lake with my face, I let go of the rope and my life jacket rocketed me to the surface. Although I can already sense just how dramatic this is going to sound as the sentence forms in my brain, I'm going to share it anyway—as I broke through the surface and gasped for air, I had the sense of being... *reborn*.

The jig was up. My teenage, high school facade/image would never again hold water (bad pun). Like so many kids, then and now, during that period in my life, I thought I had to be something, *be somebody*, and so I made up this character, crafted by what I believed to be most desired and worthy. I played that character passionately, much to the detriment of honoring who I really was (which of course was still unknown to me at the time).

It would be a bit audacious to call it an "enlightenment experience," as it was also cloaked in a heavy dose of embarrassment. I'd spent a good deal of time and effort developing this character, after all, and now there was a significant crack in the armor.

The words of philosopher Benjamin Blood occurred to me:

"There is a crack in every thing that God has made; but through that crevice enters the light of heaven."

Who doesn't love a good crack?

Letting go of that rope led to letting go of the contrived and cultivated image of myself, and many additional beliefs as well. I decided not to play football anymore, as I realized I had long ago lost any enjoyment in it and was using it as a means to feel OK about myself. I let go of the need to do anything to feel OK, and took the risk to just BE, and see what happened.

Letting Go, Acceptance & Allowing

What is it about "letting go" that can feel so... unsafe?

What is it that we're relinquishing, exactly?

That day at the lake I dumped an identity based on shaky foundations. Maybe for you it's guilt about something you've done or should have done, or resentment over something that you sense has been done to you?

You've heard the musings and seen all the memes:

Let Go and Let God.

Let That Shit Go!

Even that Frozen Princess Elsa is telling us to *"Let it go, let it go go go go go go..."*

The messaging is consistent: if something isn't serving you, Let That Shit Go! However, most folks find letting go harder than a choirboy in a porn shop.

Which begs the question: Is letting go something we actually DO, is it an action at all?

If so, *how* the hell do we do it? And why does it seem so against our instincts? Why did I hold on so tightly to the rope when I was getting battered worse than Kevin Costner's reputation for his own aquatic beat-down disaster *Waterworld*?

The Illusion of Control

We are prone to hold onto the *known* at all costs, to avoid the uncertainty of the *unknown*, the yet-to-be-created.

How much control do you think you truly have over the external world, anyway? Personally, if I could accurately account for my well-honed confirmation bias, I'd guesstimate I have close to none. Does that seem frightening to me... yeah, sometimes it does. That's likely why I routinely forget and fantasize I have Thanos-like powers to control EVERYTHING.

And then I remember
the truth about how things work...
only to forget again, and so it goes.

During my early years of Buddhist studies, one of my favorite teachers, Cheri Huber, said *"All you must do is accept everything that you find unacceptable."* I spent a solid year with this as my single Zazen meditation focus, so we're talking *hundreds* of hours. And it was transformative.

I came to realize that acceptance
is synonymous with "letting go,"
and both are synonymous with allowing.

Acceptance = Letting Go = Allowing

Acceptance is an honest recognition of how things are in the present moment. Not accepting the present moment experience, "hanging on" or "digging in your heels and resisting"—these things don't change what IS in the present moment. The present moment will change on its own. When we resist, it persists, at least within our personal internal experience.

Acceptance isn't something we DO, it's not an action in and of itself. It is our resisting that takes active energy. We innocently put up barriers to our innate foundation of well-being, where it just wouldn't make any sense to not accept what IS.

Letting Go, Acceptance and Allowing are *not* the same as resignation, apathy, or as some people propose, an endorsement of any and all types of illicit behavior. I am not suggesting you stop taking action and doing your "good work" in the world, whatever that may mean to you, taking statues down or fighting to keep them up. I say, let the winds of your personal truth blow your skirt up over your head, and do as you are compelled.

I have found that when I desire to move energy in a certain direction, as in creating change, my track record is exponentially better when I am first and foremost in a place of Acceptance and Allowing. When I am in alignment with the present moment, I move more easily within it, and seem to have a fluid influence over it.

Ponder-ables

What gets in the way of our present moment acceptance?

What are we hanging onto?

How much control do you believe we truly have in how things turn out?

Have you ever let go of something after trying hard to control it, only to find that letting go was the impetus to the movement you ultimately desired?

CHAPTER SEVENTEEN:
BREAKING BAD (HABITS)

"Are they still considered 'bad habits' if I like them?"

When it comes to habits, their intrinsic nature and our relationship with them (including "breaking up" with them), nobody is more insightful than psychologist and 3P-based coach Dr. Amy Johnson. I highly recommend her book on the topic, *The Little Book of Big Change*, as well as her other resources (see *Resources for Further Exploration*).

In the introduction to her book she writes "...your habit is an impersonal, thought-based experience that can be addressed without rehashing your past or analyzing your life."

As my man Leonard Cohen (and a few others) have said— "Hallelujah!"

It's not about figuring out your triggers and how to navigate your entire life around avoiding them. It's not about hard-nosed discipline, because we've all experienced how discipline is great, as long as you're in a great state; but more often than not it fails us when we're emotionally off kilter even a wee bit—tired, hungry, or upset in any way. Discipline is a fickle tool that is largely unsuccessful as a long-term strategy.

Habits 101: What & Why

Dr. Johnson defines a bad habit "as any repetitive thought or behavior that one wishes to stop doing."

This is a crucial definition because it includes *habitual thought patterns* in the same way as the more common frame of habits in the behavioral realm, like biting one's fingernails, stress eating, etc. That's precisely because *thought* is the foundational basis that drives *all* our behaviors, some of which become habitual.

Our thoughts produce feelings, and then we (often) act on those feelings.

Our natural state, our home base, is one of peace and clarity, and is free of habitually driven thought patterns and behaviors. Our habits tend to show up—only show up, as a matter of fact—when we are actively THINKING about life, caught up in our minds, as opposed to simply living life.

The first step is to understand that our habits are *simply attempts to feel better*, to return to our home base state of peace and well-being.

We are all naturally drawn to return to this state. Your personal habit, whatever it may be, did indeed, at least at some point in time and for some amount of time, lead you to that more peaceful state. However, habits bring with them some unintended side effects.

And eventually,
it is the habit itself
that shifts from being
a coping mechanism
to actually
being
the
problem.

The Spiritual and Scientific Nature of Habits

Johnson has a useful way of viewing habits from both spiritual and scientific vantage points:

Spiritually: THOUGHT is the formless energy that creates our experience.

Scientifically: it is the act of thinking within the brain that is the manifestation of such an energy.

That means your thinking isn't you, and neither are the associated feelings your thoughts produce. They don't tell you anything true about you, and they're not an accurate representation of the external world. That is why attempting to force change within yourself or others is futile—we are following a fictitious map and looking in the wrong direction.

You will experience an end to your habit not from taking great action, but rather from gaining *insightful understanding.*

Again, all habits, the "good" ones, and the "bad" ones, are an attempt to *feel better.* The quality of options that appear to you at any given moment are a direct result of your current state of mind. No matter how destructive a particular habit may be, it's not "self-sabotage." You are simply doing the best you can to feel better with the available options visible from your current state of mind.

How you feel, moment to moment, is a perfect indicator of your current thinking state—calm and clear or fired up and turbulent. When you see the truth of this, for yourself and everyone, you are more able to relax. As you relax, your inner wisdom more freely comes forth to guide you. When our minds clear, when we CTFD, we naturally return to our home base, a habit-free state of being.

The Higher Brain and Your Inner Lizard

It can be helpful to imagine a distinction between a so-called Higher Brain and a Lower Brain. The Lower Brain (often referred to as the Reptilian Brain or Inner Lizard) is focused on immediate survival (and long-term survival AKA fucking, of course) and it obsessively loves routine. It has the best of intentions but isn't all that bright and cannot see the big picture. Therefore, it will latch onto anything you do (including thinking patterns) that evokes good feelings and produces urges prompting you to repeat said action over and over again. This is why so many of our habitual drivers can seem like a life-or-death scenario. Of course, this is a distorted view; it's not really about survival. But it sure feels that way, and that's why it's perfectly understandable we give in to our urges.

You act on the urges to *relieve the artificial survival tension* they create within you.

Remember this: Thoughts are impersonal.

Thoughts simply pass through you, as much as you allow them to do so. And even when you hang onto them, as we are often prone to do, they still eventually pass. When you truly begin to recognize this in action, again and again, it allows you to relax, and compassionately dismiss the feeling of urges with relative ease. No struggle needed.

This is not a technique,
it is an understanding.

When you are caught up in your habitual urges, it simply means that you are lost, lost in thought. Johnson points out that humans seem to speed up when we are lost. Most other animals stop to regain their bearings; and that is in line with the age-old advice of what to do when lost: stay put. Instead, we often forge ahead and do more, at exactly the time when slowing down and doing less would be most beneficial. When using willpower, grit, or determination, you are thinking MORE, when in fact it'd be most useful to think LESS.

What is ultimately needed to end any habit, with ease, is *insight*.

These insights are personal and look different to each of us, but at the core they are an innate understanding of the power of thought, the well-meaning but unsophisticated Inner Lizard Brain, the impersonal nature of passing thought, and the realization that our home base is a place of peace and well-being.

When you see, and innately understand via insight, that your habit is simply thought, when you see *through your habit*, if you will, it begins to lose power over you. It never actually had any power over you, and that becomes abundantly clear. Understanding the origin and purpose of your habitual urges is the first step, and maybe the only step needed to change your perspective and relationship to your habit.

The most beautiful element of this understanding of thought, habits, and your true self state, is that you'll relinquish your current habit and be unlikely to pick up another one in its place. Unfortunately, this happens all the time. You might be "upgrading" to a less destructive habit, but you're still ultimately stuck. Like the alcoholic who quits drinking smuse-juice but now slurps down two pots of coffee a day, or starts smoking cigarettes, or exercises for four hours every day, or whatever. Most of the addiction support groups are singularly focused, i.e., "Alcoholics Anonymous," "Narcotics Anonymous," or "Overeaters Anonymous." What about one called "Addictions Anonymous," which would look towards the nature of all addictions. After all, the fundamental nature of all habits is the same. It's always based on a simple misunderstanding.

And it
always
limits
choice.

The Three Steps to End Any Habit

(These should come as no surprise)

1) Notice
2) CTFD
3) Do Nothing

The (non) act of Doing Nothing is a chance for your Higher Brain to evaluate both the situation, as well as your Inner Lizard's claim that your survival is at stake. (It never is.) The true value is in the *intention* to pause and do nothing, whether you then act on your urge and do your habit or not. Over time, this type of pause will become your default, it will simply be what makes sense to you based on your understanding. You have inner wisdom you can turn to, although sometimes you won't. That's not a big deal, unless you think it is. Your wisdom will still be there for you, always.

Again, you don't need to do anything. As a matter of fact, most things you do will be counterproductive, as they're piling more thought on top of thought-created patterns.

Once you've seen
behind the curtain,
once you've poked
at the screen and
seen it isn't real,
nothing is quite ever
the same again.

Sure, you'll forget from time to time,
and then remember, and then forget,
and then rejoice upon remembering;
and that is part of the joy ride
of being a human being.

Ponder-ables

Can you sense the truth about your habits
(behavioral and mental/emotional) being
impersonal and transient?

How has a current "bad habit" been useful
to you in the past?

What if all coping mechanisms eventually
become the next problem?

CHAPTER EIGHTEEN: DIRTY GOALS

Don't half-ass anything; whatever you do in life, use your full ass.

In this essay we tackle the topic of "dirty" goals and as usual, it will likely be less fun than it sounds.

I have a love/hate relationship with traditional goals and the manner in which we approach them.

That's not entirely true, I don't actually love them at all.

And in honor of Dr. Seuss, there's no time to hate, either.

Let's just say that it pains me to see the way most people, including yours truly for most of my life, engage with goals and perpetuate our own dis-ease. Common sense might suggest that when a system of thought and behavior has a miserable success rate, like in the low-single-digit-range, it's likely *not* the fault of the participants, but rather a flaw in the set-up itself.

I suggest there is a serious design issue with the *structural dynamics* of goal setting, at least the way it is usually done.

I trust you've experienced this frustration with goals of which I speak at least once, or twice, or maybe hundreds of times? I'm going to assume most everyone has set goals in the past, and many of you are probably working towards some goals right now. Here is my question for you:

How are you *feeling* within that process?

If you're right as rain, good on you. But if you're not, and maybe you even believe that struggle is an inevitable part of the process... Yeah, let's explore that a bit.

People are taught they need to set goals, maybe they even need to follow a specific protocol. For example, what's the first thing you do? You write them down, because studies show that's exponentially more effective.

But is that really so?

One of the most cited goal setting studies is from the *Yale University Class of 1953*. These graduates were tracked for twenty years, and researchers identified a correlation between written goals and success (measured—how else?—but in annual earnings, which is an entirely separate topic). What did they find? Some of you may already know, as this is a rather famous study: the 3% of graduates who had *written* goals out-earned the other 97% of the class combined.

Holy Moly Guacamole Ravioli! That would indeed be an impressive stat—if it were true.

As it turns out, Yale has repeatedly denied the existence of any such study, as have all the other Ivy League Universities. I've heard Tony Robbins repeat this Mr. Snuffleupagus-esque study many times. Apparently, he first heard it from Zig Ziglar. Zig couldn't remember where he'd first heard it, but said that he "reads a lot."

The moral of this fictitious story—don't ever believe there is only one way to move towards what you desire; even if it is from a "study."

That is not to say you shouldn't create goals, or that you shouldn't write them down. How about we investigate a few options, try out some strategies for ourselves, and see if we get a clear net benefit? Then we can decide if we want to wash, rinse and repeat.

Most of my coaching clients arrive with goals and desires already formed and ready to go. This is all well and good. However, before diving into their perceived obstacles and utilizing their innate wisdom in how to proceed, I have found it makes sense to identify if they're in an abusive relationship with their goals. By that I simply mean if they are using the creative power of thought in unproductive ways. Have they gotten themselves all worked up in the most common misunderstanding in the world: that their own internal peace, joy, happiness, satisfaction and all the other beautiful states have a damn thing to do with the external world of form, and their ability to manipulate and bend it to their will?

I'm going to be sharing some quotes and paraphrased sections from an exceptional book titled *Clarity*, by Jamie Smart. It covers a wide range of topics from the Inside-Out paradigm, but I wanted to highlight how he breaks down this incredibly popular, and utterly dis-empowering, misunderstanding about getting what we think we want (goals) in order to FEEL what we would like to feel.

This is, in other words, a perfect example of the outside-in illusion.

The Set-Up

Smart has identified a common structure of modern-day goal setting. Here's the basic set-up. Now, stick with me because this is as attractive as it is fucked up.

I'll be _____ (internal feeling) when I _____ (do, be, experience or acquire).

Let's consider a few examples to see how this works in practice:

I'll be successful when I make a million dollars and buy a huge house with a pool.

I'll be satisfied when I can take two vacations a year.

I'll be happy when I find my soulmate.

I'll be free when I can stop dieting.

I'll be at peace when I can love and accept myself.

Did you notice we went from money and materialistic stuff all the way to the more "enlightened" outcomes of loving and accepting oneself? It truly matters not a rodent's ass how you fill in the blanks, with a 25,000-square-foot McMansion or world peace. The error is in the structure itself:

I'll be (feeling) when I have/do (circumstance).

Again, circumstances cannot create feelings (ever). Nothing external can directly cause an internal emotion.

Say it with me now: "Happiness is an inside job." I've known that for over 30 years.

You know it, too. Or do we? We know it *intellectually*, but do we have an embodied understanding of this truth?

I forget on a daily basis, especially when it involves "personal development" or "being of service to others."

For example:

I'll be a more confident coach with more training and the latest and greatest certification.

I'll be a true yogi when I can eliminate my negative thoughts.

I'll be worthy when I've volunteered enough time or built an orphanage (or whatever).

This particular trap is so attractive because it seems to offer a straightforward solution; acquire or alter something externally, and it will change how you feel internally. It's such a fine ass trap precisely because it is so attractively simple, the bait is almost irresistible.

It's just not true.

But What About...?

If you're anything like me, you can likely spit out a plethora of examples of your internal feelings seemingly being caused by an external circumstance. Although we've already addressed this a couple of times, I'm acutely aware of just how persistent this illusion can be, especially with examples like the following:

I feel at peace when I am with my cats.

I feel loved because of my spouse.

I feel confident because of my academic grades.

I feel secure because I have enough money.

I feel nervous because I have to give a speech.

I feel angry because of social injustice.

In case you are wondering, all the above inaccurate source attributions are mine. Each and every one of them seem real and valid to me at any given moment. I love my cats and my wife. I prefer to get kudos of all kinds and I would rather have more money than less. I get nervous about public speaking, and I can get all worked up when things aren't "as they should be" (according to me). That's all true. The idea that my preferences need to be catered to in order to feel the positive emotions and let go of the negative ones is simply a glitch in the Matrix.

The Distinction:
Clean Goals vs. Dirty Goals

"Dirty Goals" are structured in the format above. We are looking to *feel better* by way of manipulating an external stimulus, doing, or acquiring something. I hope I've presented enough material as to why this set-up is doomed for anything other than a short-lived emotional reprieve.

Clean Goals aren't bogged down with the baggage and responsibility of generating our happiness and well-being. Setting Clean Goals is also easier and a shit-ton more fun. You already know you are whole, more than enough, better than OK, right as you are in this moment. And then, from there, we can ask ourselves:

"Now, what cool shit do I want to do, create or have?"

Can you feel the difference?

Here are two common results I've noticed shifting from Dirty to Clean Goal Structures:

1) *Goals often change.* This can be shocking for people who have had a particular long-term goal, sometimes for decades, to suddenly realize it's not really what they wanted; they simply wanted the feelings they thought their goal would give them.

Now that they have those feelings, without having achieved that goal, they are drawn to go in a different direction.

2) *Success rates skyrocket.* When we are clean with our goals, we don't have the stories around success or failure of said goal. This is experienced as freedom, and a lightness, as opposed to the pressure and weight of needing the external success in order to be OK. In my experience, everyone optimizes their potential to a greater degree when they are free.

The best part:
even if you fail
you're still OK.

Failure is Always an Option

To be clear, when I suggest that with clean goals it doesn't matter (in the grand sense of things) if you fail to reach your goal, some people get their knickers in a knot over the word "failure." As in, "there is no such thing as failure," or "failure isn't an option."

I appreciate the power of language. I love words and often use (and perhaps abuse) them to my advantage and for entertainment. "Re-framing" is a useful technique made popular decades ago through Neuro-Linguistic Programing (NLP) and other personal development programs.

However, in relative reality, if my goal is to run twenty miles, and I only run twelve before I have to stop due to a severe case of the Hershey-Squirts—call it what you will, but I failed to run the twenty miles. The beauty of a clean goal is I don't have any attached story about what it means that I bailed at only twelve miles. I can be disappointed about this failure, but a bit of disappointment is just that, a bit of disappointment. Like all feelings, it will pass through me at a rate directly proportional to my allowing it to do so.

The ever-popular self-development question, "What would you attempt if you knew you could not fail" is fine. I find a more interesting version to be:

What would you attempt if you knew it was perfectly OK to fail?"

Ponder-ables

Imagine you already have every positive feeling you desire, what would you THEN want to do, create, or have?

What would you attempt if you knew it was perfectly OK to fail?

SECTION IV:
SPIRITUAL ENEMAS

CHAPTER NINETEEN:
ON BEING CALM
AND CONFUSED

"George Washington was in a cult, and that cult was into aliens, man."
 —Slater, Dazed & Confused (1993)

Dazed and confused. We've all been there. Some of us more often than others, no doubt.

While there seems to be marginal to zero benefit in being merely dazed, I believe most of us have an unjustified aversion to the mental/emotional state of confusion. This aversion can elicit concern, at least initially, from some of my coaching clients and perhaps any reasonable person reading this book or listening to my podcast, *There is No Spoon*.

Let's explore the space where the states of *calmness and confusion* cannot only coexist peacefully, but rather how this seemingly odd combination (kinda like putting wasabi on a hot dog—highly recommended) creates a ripe environment for insights.

Before I share why I personally adore this particular feeling/state combination, it might be interesting to ponder why so many of my clients seem to experience mild confusion during our sessions or listening to the podcast.

First, the subject matter itself, who we truly are and how our experience of life is created, is an esoteric topic.

Second, the way in which we are pondering the subject; that is, at a meta-level, the *nature* of thought itself. (More on that in a moment.)

Finally, we are attempting to explore and share ideas via words (form) about something beyond the material realm (formless).

That's a triple whammy headshot to any chance of total clarity—at least within the thinking mind.

You Put a Spell on Me?

Another clue may be gleaned from an observation of a good friend named Sam, who is rather gifted in the art and science of language and communication skills, including NLP and Therapeutic & Conversational Hypnosis. Upon listening to several of my podcast episodes, he was impressed with how I had structured the shows to allow for conversational hypnosis patterns to be fluidly embedded, my use of nested loops and the subtle invitations to enter into transderivational searches. He guessed my listeners were likely experiencing light trance states throughout the episodes.

Just in case you're not an NLP or Hypnosis geek, let me define a few terms.

Nested Loops are a technique utilized in some forms of conversational hypnosis where the practitioner will intentionally start but not finish several stories (called open loops) and then ultimately bring them to a conclusion near the end. Sort of a big crescendo, if you will.

Transderivational Searching is something we all do whenever someone is speaking, or however we may be presented with new or novel information, and we "go inside". That is, we do a search within our existing database of knowledge to make sense of this new information by comparing and contrasting it with stuff we already know.

This creates what can be termed a *light trance*, in that you are changing mental states by changing your focus. "Trance" simply refers to the process of transitioning from one state to another.

As much as I would love to be able to take credit for having set up such an elaborate structure to my episodes, that would be some egoistic BS, and quite frankly, I'm just NOT that clever. Nested Loops, in particular, are more an art than a science, both subjects that I barely managed to pass in high school.

However, I do purposefully move from the specific to the general or abstract, as I'm much more interested in what is true for all of us human animals than simply what appears to be happening to me, or you, in the moment. So, by "going abstract," most of you will, by default more than by my design, launch into your own transderivational searches.

Naked Listening

There is a good chance that these types of topics, addressed in this manner, will induce a light trance state. Many people find this calming, while also a tad bit confusing. Which is why I suggest "naked listening." That's not to say without clothes, unless that is your preference, *and* it won't get you arrested. Rather, I mean without any mentally straining attempts to agree or disagree and/or compare/contrast the concepts and perspectives with those you already know and understand.

Sam went on to ask me if I was at all concerned how many of my listeners were actually "getting it," what it was that I was *really* saying, on the level to which I was pointing. My answer surprised him a bit, and I suppose it might surprise you as well, which is that I have ZERO concern about it.

That's right, none at all.

I'm not concerned that you get exactly what I'm saying or that you have any particular experience in the moment while reading or listening. It's not that I don't care about you and your journey. I'm just not invested in *how* and *when* you come to understand your True Nature and become free. I have total faith you will. It's inevitable. Your personal journey is yours to have at your own pace. You can decorate it to suit your personal taste.

This is in sharp contrast to the way I used to coach, when I utilized techniques like NLP, Time-Lines, EFT and the like. If you came into a session and you had a subjective rating of 8/10 for anxiety about someone or something, I would figure out which tools and techniques to use to get that down to a much lower level, often to a 0. I will admit that was a fun way to coach, and it does have some value. It's just not what I do anymore. It began to seem like clients were seeing me and my "tricks" as key to their feeling better. Once a person *needs* a technique or someone else, it sets up the potential for misunderstanding and a false dependency and moves one away from personal freedom.

These days I am simply looking to share perspectives, connect, and create a space with ripe soil for fresh, new insights to sprout. These insights don't need to come forth within a session, while listening to an episode or reading this book. They also don't need to be seen in the same way that I happen to be seeing things at the moment. I am not invested in exactly HOW anyone lives out their lives, or what meanings they ascribe to things. That's not a concern of mine. Everyone will awaken and get what they get when they get it. This may be impacted—or not be impacted at all—by my interaction with them. I trust that each person can get grounded, and that wisdom will reveal itself, moment to moment.

The Meta-Level Nature of Thought

Clarity Coach Founder Jamie Smart has a useful approach to our understanding of—and relationship to—Thought.

There are three distinct aspects:

First, you have the CONTENT of THOUGHT

Here we evaluate the literal "stuff" of your current thinking, and then go about amending it with strategies and techniques. These might include positive thinking or affirmation protocols. Most of us who have been around the "self-improvement" rodeo a few times have tried countless variations on this theme, i.e., you have a "bad thought" and instead you think about bunnies, or you stand in front of a mirror and repeat, "I am calm and confident," over and over (regardless of how you are actually feeling in the moment).

Second would be the STRUCTURE of THOUGHT

This category includes strategies like NLP, CBT, EFT etc. These are interesting tools in that they allow you to "fuck with" (technical term) how you are interpreting and experiencing your thoughts. You can reframe a past situation, quell the emotional impact, or tap them away (semi-literally), to name just a few of your choices here.

Finally, we have the NATURE of THOUGHT

This is where these sorts of wondering, pondering, meta-level inquiries are always headed. Sure, we take several detours while on this journey. Who hasn't gone 45 minutes out of the way while driving cross-country to see the World's Third Largest Ball of String? But our compass will always be showing us True North, which is towards our True Self.

What is the nature of thought, exactly?

- originates from an unknown origin
- will flow through you at precisely the rate it is allowed to do so
- is impersonal

It truly is that simple, as is the path to freedom that is available from this embodied understanding.

In my experience,
a calm mind is likely to be open,
and when you are
simultaneously confused,
you are standing
at the gateway
between the known
and the unknown.

All potential creation lies in the unknown, and all we have to do is step forward into it with faith and perhaps even, dare I suggest, excitement, because it is in this state that you can genuinely ponder...

I wonder
what I'm about
to discover.

Ponder-ables:

What is your experience of Naked reading or listening? The next time you are in conversation with someone, can you simply listen with full attention, without actively trying to make sense of what is being said, or how you will respond?

Can you loosen and perhaps redefine your relationship with the state of confusion? Instead of a problem to be solved, might it be experienced as the precursor to the arising of your Innate Wisdom?

The Nature of Thought: unknown origin, impermanent (flows through us), and impersonal (it doesn't mean a damn thing about you, other people, or your current circumstances).

CHAPTER TWENTY:
EGO IS NOT THE ENEMY

"Ego is a social fiction for which one person at a time gets all the blame."
—Robert Anton Wilson

What If We Declared a War and the Enemy Never Came?

Many of you will be familiar with the work of Ryan Holiday, whose books include *The Obstacle is The Way, Stillness is the Key,* and of course, *Ego is the Enemy.* Now, I hate to take issue with a writer I truly admire, but from my vantage point, this last title is a bit off the mark and potentially leads us down a shit-filled rabbit hole.

I'm just going to come right out and say it: I don't think the Ego is a thing. I don't believe it exists. I get why it's an attractive idea. I mean, we always seem to need a bad guy. It could be a "bad gal" if I want to be all PC, and occasionally that may be the case, but us guys seem to have captured a good deal of the market by playing the villain.

This need for a bad guy plays out in almost every genre. We see it in overtly fictional stories for entertainment, politics (which are basically fictional stories), the news (again, fiction), sales copy and advertising (I trust you see the fictional trend here). The chosen scapegoat for our dis-ease doesn't even need to be a human, it can be something as existentially benign as a receding hairline. And then we take the ever-popular action of "going to war" against this illusionary opponent, be it another country, drugs, poverty, religion, science or what have you.

We've
gotta
have a
bad guy.

The first step is to identify the bad actor. (I'm *not* referring to Nicholas Cage. Leave my main man alone; he killed it with epic performances in *Wild at Heart*, *Adaptation* and *Pig*. I believe Cage intentionally does one great film every decade, and total shit work in between, primarily to provide contrast... but it's just a working theory.)

The next step is to develop an attack plan to kill him. Regarding killing the Ego, this is usually undertaken in what might be called the psycho/spiritual domain. And although it is sometimes classified as a war against the ego, more often than not these "spiritual soldiers" use phrases such as transcending or releasing the ego, or "self-surrender," as this type of terminology sounds less violent and more spiritual-ish.

Richard, Ralph, Tim & The Tibetan Book of the Dead

Timothy Leary is credited with coining the term "ego loss," considered synonymous with "ego death," in the context of psychedelic journeying. I was first introduced to such adventuresome ideologies while studying Comparative Religions at The California Institute of Integral Studies in San Francisco. To call it a hippie school would be a masterpiece of an understatement. Seriously, we sat in circles on the floor and performed a group meditation before every lecture. The library also had an entire bookcase dedicated to gobbling entheogens for enlightenment.

I was intuitively drawn to what might be considered the bible of such books, *The Psychedelic Experience: A Manual Based on the Tibetan Book of the Dead* by Timothy Leary, Ralph Metzner & Richard Alpert (who later took the name Ram Dass).

The original *Tibetan Book of the Dead* was used by Tibetan Buddhists as a guide to assist dying persons through the experiences they can expect to experience immediately after physical death, through the different stages (referred to as *bardos*), and finally, if needed, onto the next rebirth, hopefully in an upper-level vehicle (i.e., a human as opposed to a duck-billed platypus).

The Psychedelic Experience manual is intended to guide one through those stages of the Tibetan Book of the Dead. But instead of the *physical* death of the body, you experience a temporary death of your ego. You get a glimpse into the Void, spiritual emptiness, no-self.

The book was equally frightening and comforting. You are instructed on what to expect, the most favorable ways to react, and how it's very much like a box of chocolates. I suppose it could be summed up with "CTFD and let it take you where it will." To experience the death of your ego, even when it is sought after and expected, and even with the knowledge that it will only be temporary... is exciting, confusing and potentially utterly terrifying.

Heroic Doses & The Void

There I was, a few hours after ingesting what the late, great Terrance Mckenna (a sometimes-guest lecturer at the school) called "heroic doses," sitting on the edge of The Void. Perhaps "suspended" in the

Void would be a more accurate description, albeit still completely incomplete as a true conveyance of the experience. It was like I was in one of those images from deep space. But saying I was "in" something immediately falls short, because there was only one thing...
and it was Nothing
and therefore
it was Everything.

I had been exposed to this concept in my studies and had what I thought to be a solid theoretical understanding of it. And I liked the concept. I could talk about it at great length (with the ego loving every minute of it).

But it wasn't until I entered the Void and became one with it that I had any sense of what I had previously been rambling on about for years. It is only when my ego seemed to temporarily die that I realized I was nothing—not just something other than what I thought myself to be, but absolute nothingness—that the infinite potential revealed itself. For when you are nothing in particular, you are at the same time everything. Looking back now, it was certainly the closest experience I'd ever had of switching perspectives: instead of looking at the finger pointing at the moon, I was the motherfucking moon.

So, my friends, I did have that experience, and it was grand, it was transformative, and in many ways changed the course of my life. I'm damn glad I did it. However, I've come to believe it wasn't truly necessary, and it was spectacular for reasons *other* than the apparent death of this thing called Ego.

I Got 99 Problems, and an Ego Ain't One

Why do I keep referring to Ego as *this so-called thing*?

Again, because I don't believe Ego to be a real thing. It's a concept, and like all concepts, is made up of thought. "Made Up" being the operative phrase. Ego is simply a collection of thoughts we have about ourselves. It's no different than self-image—again, made up of thought. Those thoughts generate feelings, and those feelings certainly seem real. That's how it works. But those feelings are just thoughts taking form and hanging around primarily because we grab onto them.

What if it truly were that simple?

It can be tempting to categorize some self-images or egoistic senses of self to be "good" and others "bad." If you think of yourself as a shithead, you're likely inclined to feel...

shitty. Conversely, if you think of yourself as intelligent, then you might feel as such. However, when we mistake any ego-based or self-image quality to reflect who we truly are, we invite maladaptive behaviors to protect that (relatively meaningless) quality, which tends to pull us off our home base of peace and contentment.

For example, if I believe I am intelligent, and that particular quality/asset is part of my value as a human being, I will be inclined to *protect* and *defend* that part of my identity—and why wouldn't I? And the moment I move into a protective and defensive position, I am less able to hear new ideas from others, or to collaborate effectively. My misunderstanding of my true innate value has limited my overall ability to enhance said skill set (intelligence), not to mention my subjective experience of life and my relationship with others.

Of course, the more often we believe those thoughts/feelings to be real, and continue to engage with them, the more embedded they become. Those neuropathways get stronger, and we naturally default into a belief system about who we are. We have innocently created an ego or self-image house of cards that will inevitably topple at some point, hopefully sooner than later, and, if it's not asking for too much, without excessive suffering.

The Ox Suffers, the Cart Complains

There is a cool Zen parable that addresses the inevitable result of identifying with our thoughts as an indication of our identity.

A novice monk approaches the headmaster of the monastery and asks for a faster way to dis-identify with his ego-self and attain enlightenment. The headmaster instructs the novice monk to retreat to his room and meditate on an ox until receiving further instruction.

Four long weeks pass with the young monk meditating on nothing but an ox, day after day.

Finally, the headmaster knocks on his door and tells him to come out.

He replies, "I'm sorry, but I cannot. My horns won't fit through the doorway."

At that moment, the monk achieved enlightenment.

Ponder-ables

You are NOT your thoughts—not even the "good" ones.

Ego is simply an accumulation of repeated thoughts and emotions that form and perpetuate the illusion of being a separate entity.

Make love, not war with your Ego. For if you love your Ego, you will set it free. And if it comes back, well, perhaps you need a restraining order.

NOTICE

CHAPTER TWENTY-ONE: THE SPIRITUALITY OF NAKED YOGA

Yoga is not about tightening your ass. It's about getting your head out of it.

Naked yoga is a hot new trend, at least among trendy folks in trendy parts of the US. In my never-ending quest to be part of the trendy crowd, I decided to go straight from no-yoga and jump headfirst into naked yoga. Sure, I could have attended a couple of the more traditional classes where your fellow peeps have their naughty bits covered. But screw the middleman! I decided to go "balls out."

You likely have many questions, such as:

Why would anyone choose to do yoga in the buff?

Is "Naked Yoga" just code for an orgy?

When does everyone strip down?

Do the Gospel Pipes and Winnebagos just flop around everywhere?

And finally, and perhaps most importantly, *should you make an anal bleaching appointment before your first class?*

Fear not, for I had these questions and many more, and attended several naked yoga classes to find out. Consider this odd essay my take on Gonzo journalism. (Indeed, many people would consider this entire book just that.)

Before we take our proverbial clothes off and get busy, perhaps a few side notes are in order:

Side Note #1: There is nothing new about Naked Yoga

Yogis have been giving the Gods the brown eye in Downward-Facing Dog since ancient times. This was especially prominent in the practice of Nagna Yoga. More recently, the puritanically influenced countries have exhorted their peeps to cover their junk, but that's not necessarily keeping true to the spirit of yoga.

Side Note #2: The Postures are NOT Yoga

When I stated I went straight from no yoga to naked yoga, that wasn't entirely accurate. Truth be told, I've been practicing yoga for almost three decades, just not the physical postures, AKA *asanas*.

Despite what many people throughout the US and Europe may think, yoga is not just twisting yourself into a pretzel or doing headstands. The asanas are actually a very small percentage of what constitutes the Eight Limb System of Yoga. Technically speaking, I suppose they're a mere 1/8th of the practice of yoga.

The first two limbs of yoga are the *Yamas* and the *Niyamas*. They are all about purification and renunciation, including compassion, truthfulness, non-stealing, sense control, and non-possessiveness; then, discipline, contentment, self-study, and spirituality. It should be self-evident why most people choose to skip these initial steps, and leapfrog to limb number three—the physical asanas.

Finally, limbs four through eight are more advanced meditation techniques. The original benefit to be derived from the asanas was to be better able to sit in meditation for prolonged periods of time.

But wait, what about getting toned and ripped, and showing off all your expensive yoga gear?

More on that in a minute...

Benefits of Naked Yoga vs. Clothed Yoga

I was unable to locate any scientific studies specifically addressing the benefits of practicing yoga poses in the raw. One could reasonably conclude that the numerous health and emotional benefits that have been documented from yoga in general would also apply when doing it wearing only a smile. These would include improved flexibility, strength, deeper breathing, and accessing meditative states, to name just a few.

The real question is, does Naked Yoga have *additional* benefits compared to Clothed Yoga?

After speaking to dozens of seasoned students, it became apparent a big draw is to gain a greater appreciation of and love for their own bodies.

Negative body image disorders are rampant throughout the US and are increasing in other parts of the world as well. Some studies report up to 8 out of 10 women are unhappy with their bodies, and as many as half of them have a "distorted" view of how they truly look. Although men seem to fare better in their self-evaluations, the percentage of men who are unhappy about their bodies is also on the rise.

One might think for people with negative body image issues, stripping down in a room full of strangers would be horrifying. Many students confirmed this to be the case. However, like so many things in life, the idea of something can vary greatly from the actual experience of it. A common side effect of an Outside-In Misunderstanding, if you will.

People consistently reported that after the initial disrobing and the subsequent (although short-lived) panic, they were shocked to find a peaceful ease to the whole scene. One woman ascribed this to finally seeing *real* human bodies, as opposed to the fake airbrushed images that bombard us all the time through the media.

After all,
beneath our clothes...
we're all naked.

This can foster a sense of connectedness with and compassion for others. Perhaps even oneself.

Naked Yoga & Freedom

Apart from any body image issues, Naked Yoga seems to offer many participants an overall sense of freedom.

To test this out for myself, I attended several

traditional (clothed) yoga classes, so I could discern any noticeable differences. To be as consistent as possible, I went to classes taught by the same instructors who led the Naked Yoga classes. As I reported back from the field, I did feel a greater sense of openness and freedom *sans* clothing. It's challenging to put this subjective feeling into words, but it was pronounced and... I guess I'd say... refreshing?

Naked Yoga & Anti-Materialism

What drew me personally to Naked Yoga was the aspect of anti-materialism inherent in nudist activities in general, and in Eastern spiritual pursuits in particular. Nakedness has a long history in the ascetic traditions of various world religions. During my graduate studies I became enthralled with Jainism. What initially intrigued me was their extreme stance on *ahimsa* (non-violence). Later I came to appreciate their ascetic practices, both because of their diligent stance, as well as the deep spiritual meaning and significance underlying them.

Still to this day, in many parts of the world, if you see a dude wandering around naked with no possessions, there's a chance he's a Sadhu, one who has renounced the material world for spiritual pursuits. This is a path I greatly respect, although I have come to believe it isn't necessary... But I'm wrong about most things, so the jury is still out.

If you haven't noticed, yoga has become big business in first-world countries. In the US alone, one study found Americans spent over 16 BILLION (with a friggin' B) dollars in a recent year on yoga classes, clothing, and gear.

And since we're talking about Naked Yoga, let's focus on the clothing element for a moment.

From what experienced yoginis tell me, it's commonplace for women to wear $200–$300 worth of specialty yoga clothing to a class—and many of them have several such outfits. Designer labels abound, the inanest being Lululemon. Lulu is so easy to pick on not only because they're one of the biggest and most overpriced, but also because, despite their brilliant marketing, they're probably the LEAST yoga-like company on the planet.

I'm not one for ranting, or so I tell myself, so if you're interested as to why I'm shitting on Lulu in particular, do a bit of Internet research on Lulu and child labor sweat shops, racist humor in the naming of the company, and their obsession with *Atlas Shrugged*, just for starters. Be forewarned: it's quite a rabbit hole.

For some people, their clothing is just a form of "signaling," or a way to differentiate themselves from others. Differentiation is a method of further solidifying the illusion of separation between oneself and other people, and even all of nature. This is in direct opposition to the original intent of yoga practice, which is non-duality or union. The word *yoga* is derived from the Sanskrit root *yuj-*, meaning "to join" or "to yoke" or "to unite."

Clothes make the man
(or woman), or so they say.
What is left when all
clothes are forsaken?

Remember, we're all naked under our clothes.

Just the Facts, Ma'am

It just occurred to me I may not have answered some of the initial questions, so here goes:

Why would anyone choose to do Naked Yoga?

I think I covered that one: body acceptance, freedom

Is "Naked Yoga" just code for an ORGY?

Not in my experience. But you never know, so do your research, as your mileage may vary.

When do you strip down?

Everyone got naked at the beginning of class, when the instructor said "OK, let's get naked."

Do the Gospel Pipes and Winnebagos just flop around everywhere?

Yep, in some poses more than others.

Should you make an anal bleaching appointment before your first class?

Well, this one is optional. I chose to do so, but primarily for research purposes to assist my best friend with his first novel, *Zen and the Art of Anal Bleaching: A Back Door Journey from Darkness to Light.*

Ponder-ables

What is your current relationship with your body?

What might you be hiding under your clothes?

Might there be something seriously wrong with Stephen?

CHAPTER TWENTY-TWO:
ON BEING HEAVILY MEDITATED

"If it weren't for my mind, my meditation would be excellent."

—Pema Chodron

To meditate or not to meditate?

For many people, that seems to be the question.

Some of these many people ask me if I have a personal meditation practice. I do. In fact, I meditate almost every day. Over the past thirty years I've experimented with dozens of formal meditation practices from Zazen to Transcendental Meditation to Vipassana to Loving Kindness and many others. In this essay, let's explore formal meditation practice, its potential value and its well-camouflaged traps in which many seekers become ensnared—myself included, many times—and finally, the idea of a "quiet mind."

Shh... You'll Be Smarter in a Moment

Speaking of "quiet," I am a long-time fan of silent meditation retreats. It's funny how people are often utterly amazed, intrigued and/or confused by the idea of silent retreats, and why people would choose to do such a thing. I'm asked if it's tough not to speak for an entire week or two.

Truth be told, the hard part is integrating back into all the noise of everyday life.

For example, one evening on a silent retreat at The Omega Institute, there were about thirty of us sitting on a hillside after the last meditation session for the night. It was about 10:00 PM. Out in Rhinebeck, NY there's minimal light pollution, so the stars and planets look so damn big, almost pregnant, like you could just reach up and squeeze the juice right out of them.

We're all there together, but vowed to silence, so we're able to take it all in. Without that commitment to silence, out in the "real world," people would likely screw it up by saying something like, "Wow, would you look at that!" or the ever-popular comparison protocol, which would be something like, "Damn, this night sky is beautiful, but the most beautiful by far was back in 1987 when I was in Hawaii and blah, blah, blah." Of course, this person would have meant no ill will and was likely just trying to connect, so I'm not suggesting we castrate them, but that's what I really love about silent retreats.

You see, silence itself is a form of meditation. It sets the stage for a quiet mind, which we'll address here shortly.

Know Your Why & the Risks

The key distinction for me these days is the REASON I meditate. I used to meditate in an attempt to quiet my mind. Now I meditate simply because I dig it; there is no end goal, such as a certain state of mind that I'm looking to achieve (although often my mind does indeed get quiet). However, it doesn't always happen that way, which is now fine with me.

I have a couple of reservations when it comes to practices or techniques designed to quiet the mind or alter your mental/emotional state in any way. The first one is that people can become dependent on them. Meditation just becomes one of their Adult Teddy Bears.

For example, I work with a lot of athletes (mostly golfers) on their mental game and developing a spiritual approach to their chosen sport. Golf can be brutal from a psychological standpoint. Most sports have one or more reactionary components, which don't allow much time for thinking and therefore rely on intuition, reflexes, and instincts. But golfers must initiate every action themselves and spend the majority of every round alone in their heads between shots.

I was coaching a golfer who was looking to make it on the professional tour, and she had developed what she believed to be a reliable pre-round mental game routine, including a 30-minute meditation with visuals, breathing and other techniques. This had been quite effective over the course of the past year. That was, until the first day of Q-School—that's "qualifying school" for you non-golfers out there. It's a big deal. On that day she was an hour behind schedule, due to no fault of her own, and had less than 9 minutes to do her 30-minute pre-round protocol. Believing the formal meditation practice was what she *needed* to get into her optimal mental state (and that she had to be in such a mental state in order to play well), she panicked. No surprise—she played poorly and missed her chance until the following year.

If you have a practice you believe you *must* perform in order to attain a desirable state of mind, and you need that state of mind to perform well, then you are always at risk. Even if your practice worked 100% of the time—and no practice does—you are still at risk of simply being unable to perform it due to any number of variables outside of your control.

However, when you have the insightful understanding that all feeling states are generated by thinking, you know you are always but one thought away from a completely different mental/emotional state.

Furthermore—and this is rather contrary to most sports psychology mantras out there— you'll also realize you don't have to worry about being in your ideal mental/emotional state to perform at a high level. You may not be totally "feeling it" in the moment, but when that doesn't lead to stress and panic, athletes find they can still kick ass regardless of the quality of their current mental state.

Meditation Isn't an Olympic Sport

My second caution would be for people who inadvertently get so fixated on attaining mastery of the formal meditation practice that the mastery itself is the goal, i.e., to become a "rock star meditator." Most people begin a meditation practice for the benefits it provides, which include a feeling of being centered, peace of mind, a mind/ body connection, less stress, and the like. Somewhere along the line, many of them lose sight of that, and instead begin to focus on how well they are doing (or not) instead of the practice itself.

This is a crucial shift away from one of the most valuable teachings of meditation,

Self-Awareness
(the truth of who and what we are),

and instead towards

Self-Consciousness
(how am I doing?)

If the primary goal of a meditation practice is a "meditative state of mind," there are a myriad of ways to get there, formal meditation practices making up only a small percentage. For example, any activity or environment that is conducive to having less on your mind will evoke a meditative state, such as walking in nature, exercising, leisurely driving, showering, playing with animals, playing with yourself (you know what I mean).

You've got a lot of options, so choose one or more that you enjoy, and that may or may not include a formal sitting practice.

How Quiet Need You Be?

I want to address the ever popular and horribly elusive state of "a quiet mind."

Most people take this quite literally (which many teachers intend), but I find such an approach limiting at best and downright disheartening at worst. Have you ever tried to get rid of all content of your mind? How did that serve you? Were you able to succeed, for maybe an entire 30 seconds or so?

Of course, you can distract your mind with mantras or by focusing on your breathing or a candle or any other object of choice. But that doesn't really mean you've got a totally quiet (as in completely *empty*) mind. And I'm going to suggest that perhaps it's not the most worthwhile goal, or at least the most helpful way to define "a quiet mind" in this context.

Instead, I'm going to propose that a quiet mind is simply a mind that has some *space*. That is, just enough space where fresh thoughts, insights, and ultimately wisdom can unveil themselves to you.

You may know of the famous Zen parable of the overflowing teacup. It goes something like this:

A PhD professor of Eastern Religion gets a private audience with a legendary Zen Master. He bows, takes a seat on a cushion and requests that the Master teach him the Truth. However, before the Master can utter a single syllable, the professor begins to word vomit all the knowledge that he has already accumulated, on and on for over 20 minutes.

At the first opportunity, the Master quietly interrupts and suggests they discuss this topic over tea. He begins to pour tea into the professor's cup and as it reaches the brim, he continues pouring. The tea is running all over the table and onto the professor's pants, at which point the professor exclaims, "Master, what are you doing? It's full, no more can fit in there!"

The Master replies, "Yeah, no shit, just like no wisdom can fit within your mind so full of intellectual knowledge."

For the record, Zen Masters are legendary for using profanity for teaching purposes. Why do you think I'm so keen on Zen?

Now, there are plenty of ways to interpret this story, the most popular one being that one must let go of or *unlearn* so much to be open and receptive for wisdom. Fair enough. However, I don't feel it's necessary or useful to believe one must completely clear the mind—as we discussed earlier, good luck with that. Instead, just have a bit less going on up there. That's all it takes to create a little space for wisdom. And anything you do (or not do) that moves you towards a meditative state of mind, will create that opening, however small, for insights to enter.

That is
indeed
all it takes.

As I've said many times already, once you get a glimpse of the Truth, you are on the path, and your final destination is inevitable. It's just a matter of time. Be patient, you are not the boss of time, and it's a made-up concept anyway.

Ponder-ables

Why do you meditate?

Do you find yourself in a state of "Self-Awareness" (the Truth of Who You Are) or "Self-Consciousness" (how well you are doing)?

What other activities do you find evoke a meditative state of mind?

CHAPTER TWENTY-THREE: LET'S TALK ABOUT FIGHT CLUB

"Welcome to Fight Club. The first rule of Fight Club is: you do not talk about Fight Club. The second rule of Fight Club is: you DO NOT talk about Fight Club!"
                                    —Tyler Durden

Whoa, Nelly.

What is this... a movie review in the middle of an anti-self-help, pseudo-spiritual book?

Yep.

I mean, it's not as if I haven't already broken just about every "best practice" for authors regarding format, structure, subject matter and general decency, right?

I love movies, both for pure entertainment and as metaphors for life. *Fight Club* is a spiritual punch in the face, so keep your dukes up and let's ponder upon the interwoven messages of this film regarding Buddhism, an Inside-Out perspective, and even a sneak peek into Non-Duality.

Zen & The Art of Fight Club

I popped my *Fight Club* cherry on Friday, October 29th, 1999.

And yes, it was quite good for me. Thank you for asking.

My utter and truly unreasonable fascination with this film was certainly enhanced by the fact that I had been deep into the study of Zen Buddhism over the previous five years. I recall every scene representing a teaching from the Zen tradition.

Within the trendy Buddhist communities and hipster movie crowds, the interplay between *Fight Club* and Buddhism was no secret. Director David Finch as well as both Brad Pitt and Edward Norton mentioned it several times in interviews.

My intention is not to recap or review the movie in a purely sequential format. Instead, I'll hit on a few major themes as they relate to Zen, the Inside-Out Understanding, and the direction in which we've been looking.

If you've never seen the film (WTF?), then stop whatever you're doing and watch it now... seriously.

If you saw it more than five years ago, it might also be a good idea to see it again ASAP.

Caveat One: If you haven't seen the movie and are concerned that it is overly violent, I hear ya. I'm a bit of a sensitive snowflake about most violence in movies. Believe it or not, *Fight Club* does have several scenes that involve, well... fighting. And it can get intense. However, it's *not* just for the sake of being gratuitous; violence serves a specific purpose in the film. That being said, there are three scenes I fast forward through each time I rewatch it (about thirty times or so by now).

Caveat Two (SPOILER ALERT): Also, if you haven't seen the movie yet, some of what follows might not make much sense unless you know that Tyler Durden is Jack's alter ego—they are the same person.

Topics we'll cover:

Fight Club has The Unnamed Narrator, referred to in the third person as Jack, and his story parallels that of Siddhartha (Buddha) himself. Throughout the film Jack learns (usually quite painfully) about the Buddhist teachings on suffering, rebirth, ego, the illusion of a separate self, guru, Sangha and Awakening.

Suffering

Let's start with every spiritual seeker's favorite love-to-hate topic—suffering.

Jack appears to have his life together in a traditional sense. He's a bachelor with a high-rise condo and a corporate job. However, he suffers from debilitating insomnia and a general sense of dis-ease. He's caught up in the consumerist culture and what the narrator calls "the IKEA nesting instinct."

At one point he states,

*"I would flip through
catalogs and wonder,
'What kind of dining set
defines me as a person?'"*

When his doctor won't prescribe him sleeping pills, Jack gets upset and claims, "I'm suffering here!" The doctor tells him to attend a support group for men with testicular cancer, to see what real suffering looks like. The doctor, of course, is under the popular misunderstanding that external circumstances are the cause of internal feelings, including suffering.

Nonetheless, Jack *literally* follows the doctor's directive (which was likely not intended), and while in the group, pretending to have cancer, was able to share his suffering with fellow human beings, most notably Bob. Hugging him and sobbing, Jack tells us:

"Something happened... I let go.
Losing all hope was freedom."

Jack was finally able to sleep through the night.

Jack becomes psychologically attached to these various support groups as his medicine, and all is well (enough) until Marla (his eventual romantic interest) enters the picture. Like Jack, she is a "faker" and a "tourist," and she acts as a mirror for him. He laments, "Her lie reflected my lie." Therefore, of course, he hates her, and once again is entrapped within suffering.

Tyler (again, to be clear, Jack's alter ego) continually forces upon Jack the recognition that suffering exists (The First Noble Truth of Buddhism) particularly in the memorable soapmaking scene.

After applying a sloppy kiss to the back of Jack's hand, Tyler pours lye on it and holds him down. The lye marries Tyler's saliva and begins eating away at the flesh of Jack's hand, but Tyler refuses to let go of him and encourages him to realize:

*"This is the greatest
moment of your life.
This is a chemical burn."*

When Jack attempts to distract his mind, Tyler tells him not to handle it (suffering) *"like those dead people do.... what you're experiencing is premature enlightenment. Give up... First you have to know, not fear, know that someday you're gonna die."*

Jack must accept the pain, and with acceptance the suffering will cease. Jack stops resisting, and Tyler pours vinegar over Jack's hand.

Physical pain (an external circumstance) is inevitable and oftentimes outside of our control. Suffering (internal feeling state) is optional, a product of our thinking in reaction to the external world.

Asceticism & Renunciation

Many forms of Buddhism promote both asceticism and renunciation, which can include the relinquishing of material possessions (or at least our attachment to them).

Jack/Tyler doesn't just give up his possessions, he BLOWS THEM UP. His condo explodes because he left the gas stove on. Even as he is in shock because of "what happened to him," he is aware of the meaninglessness of what is now gone:

"What an embarrassment—
a house full of condiments
but no real food.

Jack and Tyler start squatting in a dilapidated old house in a run-down and isolated part of town. It lacks a reliable power and water source. It is a true ascetic environment.

Jack stops taking care of his body, and as some ascetic paths teach, begins to cause his body intentional harm. I would put this forth as the primary goal of the fighting at this point on his path.

He is fighting himself, of course.

When Buddha first began his quest for Enlightenment, he left his family and their extravagant kingdom and lived with ascetics in the forest. He gave up everything and let his body deteriorate.

Tyler echoes this phase on the path:

"Reject the basic assumptions
of civilization, especially the importance
of material possessions....

"The things you own
end up owning you."

I would feel a bit remiss if I didn't point out that there is more to renunciation than giving up material possessions. As a matter of fact, one of my foremost spiritual teachers, Adyashanti, alludes to the fact that *true* renunciation has nothing to do with giving up your comfortable lifestyle accessories. In his book, *The Impact of Awakening,* he writes:

"Anyone can renounce things, people, places, or lifestyles. But only true renunciates renounce interest in their own minds; they renounce their ideas, their beliefs, their hopes, their conditioning, their wounds, their defeats, their victories, their pasts, and their futures. Many clothe themselves in the robes of false renunciation, but true renunciates are very rare, and very free."

Rebirth

Each night while attending his various terminal illness support groups, Jack changes his name tag; he becomes someone else. He is also reborn in those meetings in that he can let go, which in turn allows him to sleep peacefully at night.

There is a dramatic car crash scene when Tyler lets go of the steering wheel. Initially, Jack freaks out and attempts to keep the car in its proper lane. Tyler screams at him to relinquish his illusion of control and let the chips fall where they may.

Jack eventually does let go, much like with the chemical burn, and the car crashes into a ditch. Tyler then exclaims,

"God damn!
We just had
a near-life
experience, fellas!"

I suggest Tyler was implying something far more profound:

We are all reborn, moment to moment, thought to thought. We have an endless number of do-overs. Brand-spanking new blank pages are just waiting to be turned and filled with the energy of life.

Ego and the Illusion of a Separate Self

Jack lived in a high-rise condo with the marketing tagline: "The Place to Be Somebody." That's some clever sardonic spiritual shit right there.

While the Ego can be a good servant, it's an asshat as a master. It can assist you in getting around in this everyday relative reality. However, when it becomes the predominant perspective, it enhances Maya (the veil of illusion) and the idea of a separate self (dualism). The Ego is primarily concerned with its own survival, and therefore is always looking to support its value and uphold our false identity and sense of separation from others and the world.

In *Fight Club*, this search for a false identity is promoted by the marketing campaigns that brainwash people into believing they are somehow deficient and need to meet a fictional, arbitrary standard, a standard that is impossible for most of the population.

In order to "Be Somebody" you must continually differentiate yourself, and often be in conflict with everything and everyone that is apparently other-than-you. Of course, conflict (seemingly external, but ultimately internal) is showcased throughout the movie with literal and symbolic fighting.

Jack is constantly fighting himself (both mentally and physically) in the form of Tyler. Early in the film Tyler asks Jack to punch him.

Note: There's this awesome video on YouTube in which the character of Tyler has been edited out of the scene, so it is just Jack fighting himself (search video title: *Fight Club minus Tyler Durden*).

Eventually he recruits other men who are suffering and looking for meaning in their lives. The members of Fight Club come to realize freedom from their limiting Ego identifications while fighting each other as brothers.

"You weren't alive anywhere like you were there. Who you were in Fight Club was not who you were in the rest of the world."

And that's precisely the point; you weren't *anybody* in Fight Club. You were able to drop the illusion and all external signaling of your identity, and as Tyler so eloquently puts it:

"You are not your job.
You are not how much
money you have in the bank.
You are not the car you drive.
You are not the contents of your wallet.
You are not your fucking khakis.
You are the all-singing,
all-dancing crap of the world."

Guru and Sangha

Tyler is Jack's alter ego.
He is also his guru or teacher.

That's perfect because he's already a part of and "inside" him. This lines up with the Hindu concepts of Brahman and Atman, the

Christian stance that "the kingdom of God is within you," and the Buddhist saying, "If you see the Buddha on the path, kill him."

But more on that
last one in a moment.

Sangha is a Pali and Sanskrit word meaning "a community of spiritual seekers." Tyler creates his sangha in the form of Project Mayhem. The process for acceptance for prospective members is the same as many of the old-school, strict Zen monasteries in Japan. Those seeking admission are told to leave and are subjected to verbal and even physical abuse. Denied entry or shelter, and without food or water for a prolonged period, they may then be admitted into training.

After acceptance, their heads are shaved, as is common practice in Buddhist monasteries, to symbolize everyone is the same and dispel the illusion of a separate, individual self. This teaching is central to Project Mayhem, and Tyler preaches to them that they are

"not a beautiful unique snowflake but the same decaying matter as everything else."

Project Mayhem's goal, at least ostensibly, is to alleviate the suffering of their fellow human beings. Their *modus operandi* is vandalism and the eventual destruction of the symbolic structures of corporations and consumerism that keep people trapped in the illusion.

I would suggest this is a misunderstanding of how change happens.

Tyler is preaching destructive action to wake people up and set them free. This is a popular stance today and throughout history, but I would put forth that it has had marginal long-term success. I've not found destructive environments the most conducive to awakening and don't buy into the perspective that anything need change in the external world for people to become free.

Freedom is an *inside* job.

However, Tyler does have much better hair than me, so maybe you should listen to him.

And Finally, Awakening

In the final "chapter" of the film—did you know the film is an adaptation of a short novel by Chuck Palahniuk?—Jack's in a full-on fight with Tyler. He believes Tyler has gone too far and attempts to make sense of what he is experiencing and stop the destruction of all the banks and credit card companies.

He finally comes face-to-face with Tyler and begs him to call it all off. Tyler reveals the truth, that he is only a construct of Jack's mind. The fight has always been the same, just as it has since the time of the Buddha. The fight is to awaken and see through the illusion of an external world that is anything other than our own thought-created projection.

It's all Inside-Out.

Upon realizing this truth, Jack puts the gun in his mouth, says, *"My eyes are open,"* and pulls the trigger. This results in the death of Tyler, and the awakening of Jack.

If you see
the Buddha
on the path,
kill him,
indeed.

That is to say, if you fall for the illusion that there is any place other than within oneself to find the T-Word and the G-Word, Truth and God, you need only realize the guru you see is but a reflection in the mirror. You don't need to do any killing; the mirage proves itself to be formless as you walk through it.

Jack survives the self-inflicted gunshot wound and he and Marla live happily ever after...

Ponder-ables:

What are you waiting for... go watch the movie!

CHAPTER TWENTY-FOUR: THE COSMIC JOKE

"A serious and good philosophical work could be written consisting entirely of jokes."
—Ludwig Wittgenstein

My maternal grandmother was semi-affectionately known as "Large Marge"; the large part was in reference to her persistently dictatorial personality and was in stark contrast to her diminutive physical stature. It was a regular occurrence for her to lose her reading glasses and subsequently tear the house apart room by room searching for them, only to finally realize they were atop her head the entire time.

Upon such a discovery
we would all have a good laugh.

This absurdist ritual was more rule
than exception on any given day.

I find it quite like the spiritual journey, at least my trek thus far. We are missing something, at least it seems that way, something that will enable us to see things more clearly. We begin to search, outside of ourselves, for our missing spectacles... all to no avail.

Finally, sometimes sooner and sometimes later, we realize we possessed that which we were seeking all along. Then we remember this has happened many times before, and we will certainly not forget to look within again.

And then we do indeed forget,
and then remember; and so it goes.

Who Doesn't Love a Good Joke?

Just in case you somehow missed the slew of clues thus far into the book, I love a good joke (the more off-color and shocking the better—*The Aristocrats*, anyone?) and voracious laughter, the kind that causes you to tinkle your tights a bit and wake up the next day with a sore face and abs.

On the flip side, I also have some masochistic tendencies. I chose to study Zen because it seemed the most torturous, and I ran fifty-mile trail marathons because they promised to provide the most long-term suffering.

Like many of us, I took my spiritual pursuits seriously. I was sure that suffering was part and parcel of any True path, and so ensured it had a prominent place within my relative reality.

I gave my blood, sweat and tears to my practice.

And because, unbeknownst to me,
one thing never leads to another,
I was a regular recipient of MORE...
you guess it—blood, sweat and tears.

The more seriously I took my spiritual path,
the more serious I became in all aspects of
my life. Friends told me I wasn't laughing
as much, and I would even get the random,
"Are you OK these days?"

And then it occurred to me, an insight in
the grandest sense—

What the fuck is the point
of any spiritual practice
if not to allow you to fall
more in love
with the
experience
of life
itself?

I finally came to remember that I love to
laugh.

The brilliant Charlie Chaplin was a life-long
student of Zen (that is entirely false, but
I find him quite Zen-ish). Perhaps in part
because he was a silent movie icon, when he
did speak, it was often profound, sometimes
approaching, dare I say, the depth of Sir
Rumi. He apparently once uttered,

"In the end, everything is a gag."

Isn't that the Truth?

Timing is Everything

"Comedy equals tragedy plus time."

(a quote attributed to several sources, ranging from Mark Twain to Carol Burnett)

Comedy is all about timing, and because time is an illusion, or at the very least an artificial human construct and therefore quite bendy, we are all going to laugh about everything... eventually.

It appears laughter
is an essential element
of the spiritual end game.
But we don't have to wait for some arbitrary ending,
whether that be a full-on orgasmic Awakening or
simply the end of this current physical incarnation.
We can laugh within the only time that truly exists... NOW.

Chop Wood, Carry Water

"Before enlightenment, chop wood, carry water.

After enlightenment, chop wood, carry water."

The Zen wood/water teaching has several potential interpretations.

The most poignant for me is the bewildering paradox that "nothing has changed, but everything is different."

Our outward actions in the world may remain exactly the same, while our internal landscape has been completely remodeled. We aren't chopping wood and carrying water, all the while thinking that there must be something better to do, somewhere else we should be.

Before we Awaken, we do our shit in the world.
After Awakening, we still do our shit in the world,
butt realize that we, and our shit, are *not of this world.*

The Awakened State itself may not be a joke, per se; but to recognize, in an instant, that the divine presence we have been scouring the world over to find, was within us the entire time... THAT is some funny shit.

Ponder-ables:

Have you ever lost your (sense of) self while experiencing gut-busting laughter?

Are there examples of "tragedy" in your life that now have a comedic element to them?

How seriously do you take your spiritual pursuits?

Can you sense how that level of seriousness may affect other areas of your life?

How might you be able to chop wood and carry water while being in the world but not of the it?

SECTION V:
NEOPHYTIC NON-DUALITY

WTF IS NEOPHYTIC NON-DUALISM?

"A human being is a part of the whole, called by us 'Universe,' a part limited in time and space. He experiences himself, his thoughts and feelings as something separate from the rest—a kind of optical delusion of his consciousness."

—*Albert Einstein*

With respect for full transparency,
I am woefully unqualified
to speak on non-dualism.

Hence, this will undoubtedly be Neophytic
in nature and scope.

This is not because I haven't munched fruit
from the ND tree or savored its nectar.

I most certainly have, and it's damn tasty.

However, to speak or write
about ND is to utilize words,
and words are symbols
pointing towards concepts
which all have opposites
rendering them rather dualistic,
obviously.

Dance with paradox much?

Get used to it, for Non-Duality is nothing (or no-thing, I suppose) if not full of paradoxes. Which is, of course, itself paradoxical, as ND looks to bring into union all apparent opposites.

I dare to suggest that the intellect alone will never be able to fully grasp the essence of Non-Duality or the true extent and depth of the Ocean of Consciousness.

It is simply
the wrong
tool for such
an exploration.

I am reminded of Noam Chomsky's somewhat infamous sentence from his epic work *Syntactic Structures*:

"Colorless green ideas sleep furiously"

Now, Brother Noam was looking at syntax and semantics and other stuff way above my linguistic pay grade, but the tangential take-home for me as it relates to ND was that such a sentence is 100% grammatically correct, and equally meaningless.

And that is precisely how I feel when attempting to convey with words that which is beyond words. Praise be to Rumi and all the other mystical poets who can utilize words as mere place holders for the space between and behind the words; the space where Truth slumbers and is simply waiting for us to awaken it, to awaken to it, and to awaken within it.

Can Truth come out and play?

I don't have the gift or skill set for poetry, so we are reduced to mere metaphors and analogies. They are the only tools I have for this job, so they will have to do. Still, it's a bit like how George Burns described sex at 90 years old—"trying to shoot pool with a rope."

The best I can hope
is that I may fail
with equal amounts
of grit and grace.

Let us begin with a full face-plant failure by throwing out a couple of definitions of Non-Duality.

1) *Advaita* is from the Sanskrit roots *a*, "not"; *dvaita*, "dual." As *Advaita*, it means "not-two or "one without a second."

2) *Non-Duality* has also been described as *"the experience of intimacy with all things."* In this sense, one can lose the

feeling of separation between oneself and the rest of creation.

How Can We Experience Non-Dualism?

Some branches of Indian philosophy and religion (including Hinduism and Buddhism) consider a Non-Dual experience to be an integral element of an Awakening or the Enlightenment process, and subsequently put forth elaborate practices for achieving this elevated state. However, I am not interested in segmenting out such a universal Truth to any particular group, belief structure or set of techniques.

Furthermore, I am of the position that Non-Duality is NOT an altered state we need to somehow *get to*, but rather a simple reality we only need to *see and appreciate*.

That being said, do I believe experiencing "Unity with All Things" to be a stepping stone to what many call an Awakened or Enlightened state?

Does the Pope shit in his hat? Just to clarify, that is meant as an affirmative.

"I'll Take Metaphors for $1,000, Alex."

Within spiritual circles, the metaphoric relationship of a wave to the ocean is probably second only to the most popular weather-to-the-sky scenario. So as not to reinvent the wheel or the wave, I will simply relay it here as best I can and share how it looks to me. As usual, I will keep this as simple as I can.

There is the Ocean of Consciousness, a Sea of Being. You and me and everything in-between is included within this ocean, as a singular unit, as presence.

The True Nature (the home base) of this Ocean is when the water is still, flat, peaceful, and calm.

Energy arises from this stillness, first in the form of thoughts and subsequently as a form of identity—a sense of personal self that expresses itself as waves. These waves of thought and the identity that follows from them are transient; they arise for a time and then settle/return back to the stillness of the ocean itself.

We would never mistake a literal wave for being "other-than" the ocean from which it arose, but we do this with our thoughts and sense of a separate and distinct self

all
the
time.

It's the "optical delusion of consciousness" to which Big Al was pointing. It's how we end up seeing ourselves as cut off and at odds with nature, reality, other people, even God herself.

As if we are a wave that is somehow separate from the ocean? To see through this, to transcend the construct of dualism that can be so persistent in our minds, is to allow ourselves to surrender to our True and Essential Nature; as One, and Once and For All.

Ride the waves. Enjoy them as a symbolic expression of your unique combination of spirit and personality; and rejoice in returning to the Unity and Singularity of the Ocean of Being.

Within Relative Reality, dualism need not be something to fight against, but rather a partner with which to dance.

"Enlightenment for a wave in the ocean is the moment the wave realizes it is water."
—Thich Nhat Hanh

Can I assume that was all as clear as pea soup?

Not to worry, this is merely the introductory appetizer. The main course essays that follow will (hopefully) better satiate us.

Ponder-ables:

The "Act As If" Practice—Spend 20 minutes abiding within the "potential" truth that we are all one, that the apparent separation between us is illusory. Commit to embracing this perspective as best you can for this short amount of time. And get the hell out of the house! Go to the park or the grocery store. If this were indeed true, how does it feel? How does it alter the way you interact with "others" and with your "self"?

CHAPTER TWENTY-FIVE: NON-DUAL GRATITUDE

Gratitude {noun}: The secret to having it all is knowing that you already do.

Who here among us has taken part in some form of a Gratitude exercise, maybe writing in a personal journal, sharing in a group, or focusing in a meditation?

#MeToo

That hashtag is not to imply I was harmed by such exercises. Quite the opposite. I have found most explorations into appreciation and gratitude to be peaceful and grounding.

That is, until they began to feel forced, until they felt just a bit ass-backwards.

My Gratitude Journal Experience

At several points in my life, starting in my mid-twenties, I stumbled my way back to the practice of keeping a daily Gratitude Journal. Although the specifics have occasionally varied, the general protocol has been to write down 3-5 things, people, or experiences for which I am grateful. I have done this first thing in the morning, and tried it out as the last thing before turning in for the night.

It is a beautiful practice.

It starts out rather easy, as there is so much to be grateful for, right?

Family
Friends
Cats
Dogs
Other non-human animals
Health
Sunshine
Love
Insights
Wisdom
Laughter
Nut butters
Uma Thurman

Then, inevitably, about thirty days into a new round, I start to struggle. I begin to struggle as I start seeking to identify yet more things for which I am grateful in my life.

And seeking *always* leads me to suffering.

Yep, in my experience, even seeking gratitude ends up in some form of suffering.

Why? I believe the reason is two-fold.

Firstly, I am seeking for someone or something outside of myself that provokes the feeling of gratitude inside of me. Again, a simple misunderstanding of the origin of my feelings. And the subtle and often overlooked risk within this innocent misunderstanding is that if external creatures, objects, or events were indeed responsible for how we feel, there would always the danger of losing said creatures, objects, or events from your life, and thus our good feelings of gratitude.

What if gratitude, like every feeling (the "good" as well as the "bad"), was simply a shadow of our most recent thoughts?

What if gratitude was a space into which we can allow ourselves to BE?

What if we didn't need to find an external source to credit for our being in this *space of gratitude*?

Second, seeking specific external sources of my gratitude seems to necessitate the opposite. In other words, if I am grateful for X, Y and Z, am I therefore NOT grateful for A, B and C?

Can I be grateful for *everything*? Does that mean I cannot have a preference for some people, places, and experiences?

Here Cometh the Sun

Let there be no doubt, I much prefer sunny days to overcast, dreary ones. Like many people, I (almost) always seem to feel better on days that match my personal weather preference, and less-than-stellar on other days.

I spent some time in San Diego during college, and the weather was quite agreeable to my personality. Moving back to the Midwest was an assault on my sense of weather-related gratitude.

Would it be possible for me to prefer sunny days, while at the same time being foundationally grateful within the experience of weather itself, regardless of the current conditions? Can I feel gratitude for being part of the Ocean of Being, and all the experiential waves that arise and dissipate within it?

No Opposites, Know Freedom

Being a simple man, I often simply sit within the space of Non-Duality and ponder upon the possibility that opposites are merely an illusion. This is more of a somatic pondering than one of intellect.

It is the "optical delusion of separation" that creates the illusion of opposites.

To be clear, within the realm of day-to-day Relative Reality, opposites do exist and can be of monumental importance and assistance in navigating our way around. Red traffic lights mean the opposite of the green ones. It is good to know the distinction and act accordingly.

But we are Meta-Leveling Up here, which, come to think of it, might be a misleading phrase, as it seems to me we are actually dropping DOWN to a foundational level.

Henceforth, I will refer to this as Meta-Leveling Down (MLD).

Anyhoo, as we MLD, "opposites" dissipate altogether. That is to say, opposites only exist as concepts in the world of form (red light/green light). When it comes to the formless, which is beyond all concepts, opposites have no solid ground upon which to stand, and offer us little to no benefits.

There are no opposites of:

God
or
Love
or
Truth
or
Gratitude

Some will argue that the opposites of the above are the Devil, Hate, Falsehoods and perhaps Indignation.

Again, within the realm of *concepts*, sure. Let's explore beyond concepts, beyond labels, shall we?

As Sören Kierkegaard is purported to have shouted, "Once you label me, you negate me."

Who Would Jesus Label?

In the Sermon on the Mount, Jesus points us towards a Non-Dual perspective, free of labels, or at least noting that labels have no merit in how to treat others:

You have heard that it was said, 'Love your neighbor and hate your enemy.' But I tell you, love your enemies and pray for those who persecute you, that you may be children of your Father in heaven. He causes his sun to rise on the evil and the good and sends rain on the righteous and the unrighteous. (Matthew 5:43-48/New International Version, my personal favorite translation)

Could it be that JC was down with the ND?

How does it feel to sit in this space, a space without labels, beyond categories?

Go ahead, I'll wait.

<
<
<
<
<
<
<

In the meantime, I can sum up my experience in a single word:

Contentment.

Here in the West, contentment has a bad rap. Not sure how or why, but I am suspicious it has to do with a long-running cultural leaning towards constant improvement, always struggling to be the best, or at least the "best version of yourself." Contentment is on equal ground with laziness.

Why would one be content (satisfied in the moment) when you could be BETTER?

In some other parts of the world there exist different cultural attitudes that hold contentment in rather high regard, right up there as a natural component of Awakening itself. As we awaken from the dream, into Being, how could we not be grateful and content?

Ponder-ables:

Can you smell what Kierkegaard was stepping in—that labels negate the true essence of that to which they are applied?

Why do you suppose "Love your neighbor" is so often quoted, while one rarely quotes "Love your enemy"?

When was the last time you experienced contentment? Was it conditional on external factors?

Can you be grateful for everything, while still having personal preferences?

CTFD

CHAPTER TWENTY-SIX: THE EPIC BATTLE OF BELIEF VS. TRUTH

"Belief made no difference to the Truth."
—Diane Duane

The year was 1977. I was ten.

Truth be told, all I wanted in the whole wide world was an African American GI Joe action figure. I wanted that version specifically because it had an afro hairstyle. And DAMN did I ever want to rock an afro. (One of many dreams that will never come to fruition.)

I also had a geeky fascination with Japanese monster movies. This was lifetimes before the Internet and the infancy of even VHS tapes. The only option, at least as far as my best friend Joel and I knew, was the locally renowned Night Owl Theatre, hosted by the locally famous Fritz the Night Owl.

He wore the coolest (or so it seemed to 10-year-old boys) owl-shaped sunglasses, even though the sun had set many hours earlier and it was waaaay past a reasonable bedtime for people of any age. We instituted protocols and rituals to combat our drooping eyelids, including copious amounts of Mountain Dew and splashing cold water on our faces (this was also lifetimes before energy drinks or Wim Hof cold therapy) in our desperate attempts to stay awake for the Saturday/Sunday 12:30 AM start time of the show.

My favorite all-time Japanese monster movie—I'm embarrassed that I remember it so well—is Godzilla vs. Mechagodzilla. I would be hard pressed to tell you why, except that it was even more bizarre than most of the others; it pitted Godzilla against an alien-built mechanical doppelganger of itself.

Of course, most of these movies had the worst (but best) "special effects," including the plastic monsters destroying miniature toy cities.

Good times.

The One Truth & The True Godzilla

The battle between Truth and Belief is sorta like the one between Godzilla vs. Mechagodzilla.

Note: This is a bit of a reach, no doubt. However, I wanted to ponder on Capital-T Truth and Belief, AND I wanted to relive my nerdy monster movie youth. Believe it or not, this is the best spot for such an analogy. I ask you for a bit of leeway. But I digress...

There is only one True Godzilla, obviously.

And there is only ONE TRUTH.

The Truth is One, after all.

Let us put forth Godzilla as representing Capital-T Truth, and Mechagodzilla as representing Belief.

Mechagodzilla, like our beliefs (every last one of them), is artificial in that it was created. The aliens built Mechagodzilla in much the same way as a combination of indoctrination and cultural conditioning built our individual beliefs, which fostered our more elaborate web of belief systems (BS).

An Amicable Divorce?

Godzilla and Mechagodzilla had a strained relationship, to say the least. Likewise, the relationship between Truth and Belief can get a bit tricky and has been responsible for almost every violent confrontation throughout human history... but it need not be that way. It just takes an understanding of the difference between the two and the ability to spot Truth when you see it.

Although there are a few dead giveaways, the most reliable Truth detector is your *own grounded heart space.*

Belief can often look (and feel) like Truth, at least initially. Over time, however, beliefs show themselves to be vulnerable and ultimately transitory in nature.

In the film, Mechagodzilla looks almost identical to Godzilla. Until, that is, its outer layers are shed and the armor underneath is exposed. This is one of those telltale signs of a belief:

Beliefs
Need
Protection.

They also need us to *believe* in them. I know, call me Captain Obvious. This is an important distinction to note, however, because...

The Truth doesn't need your protection.

The Truth doesn't require your belief in it.

To take this analogy one giant Japanese monster step further,

One
can
never

believe
the Truth.

Once we "believe" the Truth, we have left
the realm of Truth and shifted to Belief. We
could say that we have effectively changed
the Capital-T to the diminutive lower-case
t-truth. This is all well and good and can
assist in our ability to chat about such
things; however, the way I see it, there is
ZERO overlap between Truth and Belief. I
love Venn Diagrams as much as the next
dork, but when I look at these two side by
side, I see no intersection area.

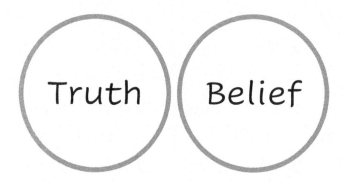

On the other foot, when instead of simply
looking/exploring, I am *seeking/searching*
(which can only occur within the realm
of beliefs), I can indeed create an illusory
intersection... and believe it.

This is the simple recipe for Bullshit: take
some element of Truth, and then believe it...

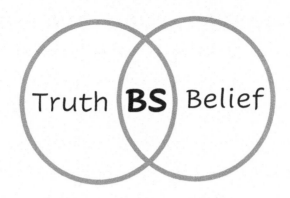

Truth **BS** Belief

When we look, with a relaxed commitment to seeing WHAT IS, the Truth will unveil itself to us; no need to get messy with beliefs.

Ponder-ables:

Are there any Truths you feel compelled to defend (from other people's perspectives or even from your own contradictory beliefs)?

What might happen if you decided to forgo that defensive position? Would your perceived Truth crumble (or change)?

Can you know the Truth of something without any thought-generated beliefs about said thing?

CHAPTER TWENTY-SEVEN: THE ONE THING

"I fear not the woman who has practiced 10,000 kicks once, but I fear the woman who has practiced one kick to the groin 10,000 times."

—Bruce Lee (heavily paraphrased, obviously)

The Hedgehog & The Fox

Do you know of this tale?

Originating from a verse by the Greek Archilochus, it has lived long and prospered thanks to a variety of thinkers and authors over many more recent years, most notably Isaiah Berlin in his essay on Tolstoy, and Jim Collins in his best-selling business book, *Good to Great*.

The basic premise: the fox is looking to make a hedgehog sandwich for lunch, and the little hog would prefer not to oblige. The fox is clever and cunning and attempts to subdue and kill the hedgehog in a multitude of ways. This effort is to no avail, however, as the hedgehog simply rolls up into itself and flares out its thorny spines, stabbing the fox repeatedly in the face.

Hence the saying, "The fox knows many things, but the hedgehog knows one big thing."

Berlin's essay on Tolstoy divided people into the categories of Foxes (those driven to have many modes of operation, interests and goals) or Hedgehogs (those having one major grounding philosophy upon which everything is predicated and evaluated).

Side Note: I read a good deal of Tolstoy in college while studying the Russian language. Why Russian, you might ask? And even if you mightn't, I will share nonetheless:

1) I thought it would look cool to be able to read a language that couldn't be sounded out by anyone studying the more "pedestrian" Romance languages (different alphabet, with several letters looking backwards—most notably the N and R). I somehow believed this elevated level of coolness would assist in getting me laid more frequently. It did not. YMMV.

2) Russian has more cuss words and sayings than most other languages. And even more, it has cuss roots, prefixes and suffixes, so you can turn any Russian word into a cuss word, fit for the exact situation where it is needed. The Russian linguist (and protest art guru) Alexey Plutser-Sarno is working on a dictionary of Russian profanity that will be TWELVE volumes in length.

But I digress...

Jim Collins put forth the argument in *Good to Great* that the most successful companies would succeed long-term by identifying their "Hedgehog Concept"—the one thing that they do the best. Although time may be telling a different story based on the current state of many companies featured in that classic book.

But alas, we are not here to wax less-than-poetic on Russian drunks or foundational philosophies of organizations. We can save those fun and fascinating topics for another book (by another author, no doubt).

The Spiritual Seeking Shotgun Approach of the Fox

When I took on my identity as a "seeker" at the age of 14, it was with a 100% fox-method orientation. I wanted to learn and practice as many paths as possible; you know, cover all my bases. It was like an endless, all-you-can eat buffet of spiritual practices, and I was that guy at the Caesars Palace free buffet that kept going back for more. I just couldn't get enough. I was busier than a cat burying poop on a marble floor.

Over time, however, it started to smell a bit like the poor fox (me) attempting to conquer and consume the hedgehog (Truth). No matter what I tried, it seemed that the more effort I exerted, the more I just kept getting turned away, continually poked in my proverbial pie-hole. It was frustrating enough to consider abandoning the journey altogether. Or at least to start drinking at a Tolstoyesque level.

Most of us have been there. You may be there at this moment. It is all good, you sexy foxes.

I eventually came to suspect that perhaps it was not *quantity*, but rather *simplistic quality* that I was missing. That damn hedgehog may have been onto something.

The One Thing That Changes Everything

I began the search for MY hedgehog, the one foundational understanding that would guide all other principles and actions.

It was a search for the Top Domino; the one that would have the cascading effect of toppling all subsequent dominoes. I was tired of dealing with the minutiae of dominoes further downstream. It was time to go upstream; time to meta-level this shit.

This time I (finally) realized that my search would be entirely internal. I would simply allow my own innate wisdom to come forth.

Side Note: I have since decided to name my yet-to-be discovered little beast "Hershel The Hedgehog." I hope that he/she/them (pronouns are such a challenge these days) is OK with that choice.

Finding My Hershel

What did my wisdom show me? What was the *one thing* that would change *everything*?

Even though I had dramatically reduced the search area by ceasing to look outside of myself for answers, there were still several top contenders, including:

- We are all worthy
- All life matters
- Everything happens for a reason
- There exists something bigger and beyond our individual self
- Jesus/Krishna/Buddha/Allah Mohammad—follow their leads
- God is love
- We are all connected

Although each of the above certainly seemed to be upper tier dominoes, they all seemed to fall a bit short of fully embodying Hershel.

And then it emerged, a simple statement that I have heard hundreds of times by a multitude of spiritual teachers and religious scholars:

We are One.

By no means a new concept to me, yet it felt fresh, enlivened as it never had before.

And as is often the case with an insight, it seemed so obvious as to be almost comical that it had taken me so long to recognize My Hershel.

We
Are
One.

Connectedness is NOT Oneness

It became apparent to me that "We are all connected" is a beautiful concept, and certainly a huge step towards Truth, but also incomplete. I came to consider it a stepping stone to the more esoteric Truth of "We are One."

Connectedness gives each of us the chance to reflect on how our actions affect others and visa-versa. It encourages compassion, empathy and the need to all get along. This is all well and good, for sure.

However, the domino that sits atop all dominoes, including connectedness, is "We are One."

The fundamental difference that makes a difference is that while connection with others encourages cooperation, it does so partially (even if subtly) through fear. Fear that without said cooperation, you or your people could be in some sort of jeopardy. It simply makes sense to play well with others, for their benefit and for your own.

Connection necessitates that there be a YOU and then OTHERS to whom you are connected.

Oneness dissolves the concept of "others." How to treat others, and the reasons for doing so, become non-issues.

Scott Barry Kaufman wrote an article in Scientific American titled, *"What Would Happen If Everyone Truly Believed Everything Is One?"*

"People who believe that everything is fundamentally one differ in crucial ways from those who do not. In general, those who hold a belief in oneness have a more inclusive identity that reflects their sense of connection with other people, nonhuman animals, and aspects of nature that are all thought to be part of the same "one thing. This has some rather broad implications."

"Some rather broad implications" is an understatement of heroic proportions.

It literally
changes
EVERYTHING.

A purely intellectual understanding and acceptance of Oneness is nice and will likely promote some changes in one's sense of being and interactions with "others." Most of us need to start somewhere, and this is a fine jumping-off point.

But to stay only within an intellectual comprehension of Oneness will never have the blessed cascading effect of an EMBODIED UNDERSTANDING of Oneness.

And this is where it can get tricky, or perhaps frustrating, to work with Oneness. I am assuming most of you, having endured this far into the book, will quite easily grasp the concept intellectually...

You sexy (and smart) foxes.

How does one move from a mere intellectual understanding to an embodied understanding? This is right up there with the all-time unanswerable spiritual Zen Koans and questions like:

What is the sound of one hand clapping?

Is a hot dog a sandwich, or is cereal considered soup?

Who the fuck knows? Certainly not me.

What I can do is share my experience of moving towards an embodiment of Oneness. Please note that I chose to use a present tense verb, as it is an ongoing and less-than-linear process.

Likely not a surprise, my suggestion is as follows:

1) Notice
2) CTFD
3) Do Nothing

Embodied understanding, at least from my current understanding, is simply your innate wisdom coming to the surface. The one requirement for this to happen appears to be SPACE. Wisdom needs a bit of room to open up inside you. And it does not seem to me that one can create space: it must be ALLOWED.

It is through allowing
that we get to accept
the grace of space.

Yep, EVERYTHING

Once embodied, Oneness changes the game completely. How could it not?

When we see *every single thing* as abiding in the Ocean of Being, we view what seems to be separateness as simply a wave; still very much part of the Whole, but just a temporary "separate" expression of itself.

We are all the same thing, and therefore despite appearances, we all want the same thing from a foundational vantage point.

Differences in political ideologies would not be seen as a problem, but simply as opportunities to see different perspectives.

You would not be inclined to steal from another wave, just as you would not withhold from a wave in need.

There would be no need for gun laws. It would never occur to you to shoot into the Ocean of Being.

Ponder-ables:

Are you a fox or a hedgehog?

Do you transform into one and then the other depending on the subject matter?

Could there be a way to marry the two, become a fox-hog: having a singular foundational grounding and an array of approaches from which to explore?

Seriously, why isn't a hot dog considered a sandwich?

CHAPTER TWENTY-EIGHT: LIFE (AND DEATH) ON THE FARM

"The greatness of a nation and its moral progress can be judged by the way its animals are treated."
— Mahatma Gandhi

I attended my first livestock auction in 1991.

My associates and I were not looking to purchase or sell. We were there to rescue and save. During the time between my bachelor and graduate studies, I had the honor and privilege of working at The Farm Animal Sanctuary in Watkins Glen, NY.

∵∵

Side Note:

I imagine that for many people, the words "farm animal" and "sanctuary" might be a perplexing combination.

Why would farm animals need a sanctuary?

Put simply, farm animals are among the

most abused creatures on Earth.

From The Farm Animal Sanctuary website:

"At Farm Sanctuary, we meet people where they are on their journey, without judgment, and model a new way to live with farm animals without exploitation of them, our shared planet, or the workers and communities impacted by an oppressive food system.

"By meeting cruelty with kindness, and treating all beings with respect, we can all demonstrate the Power of Sanctuary."

:::

Back to our regularly scheduled story...

They saw us coming from the proverbial mile away, not that we were Ninjas infiltrating the Emperor's compound, or anything the least bit insidious. Although we were bringing nothing but love, they likely perceived us as a bunch of hippies who hated all that was American, and as a threat to their incomes and way of life.

To be fair, except for being verbally abused, physically threatened, spit on and having feces thrown in our general direction, we were treated with the utmost respect.

We knew the state laws regarding the

transactional exchange of livestock. And they knew we knew the laws, which further tanked our local popularity. Most importantly, we knew it was illegal to sell an animal that couldn't walk into the showing area on its own accord, i.e. newborns birthed in transit or animals that had slipped in the trailers and suffered broken legs, non-affectionately known as "splitters."

These unsalable beings were simply thrown out back in "The Pit," although in truth it was more of a pile—of carcasses, that is. Most were still alive, although not for long without nourishment or protection from the elements. (The story occurred in the dead of winter).

If You Meet a Bodhisattva at a Livestock Auction, Take It Home

We always asked permission to take an animal. Even though they had been discarded like garbage, technically speaking, garbage was still "property." Our intent was simultaneously simple and grandiose: take the animal to the sanctuary, nurse it back to health and provide a safe, forever home.

That day it was a baby calf, maybe one or two days old, just separated from his mother, who was being auctioned as a dairy cow. I was told it was a long shot he would survive the 90-minute ride back to the sanctuary, where we had IVs, medications, and other big animal veterinarian supplies. But fuck it, we had to try. What other option was there? Simply leave him there alone to die?

I laid down beside him on the metal floor bed in the back of the pickup truck, doing my best to use my body to buffer him from the jarring bumps so prevalent on back country dirt roads.

First things first: give this being the dignity of a name to replace the numbered tag stapled to his ear. I quickly decided on Bodhi, as I had recently watched the movie *Point Break*. Bodhi was the nickname for one of the main characters, referencing the Buddhist concept of a Bodhisattva, one who forgoes Nirvana to instead show and lead everyone to enlightenment. I had a sense this young, suffering creature held within its soul an answer to a question that I didn't even know how to ask.

Not yet at least.

I struggled to get him to drink formula from a bottle. He politely refused and insisted instead on suckling three of my fingers. I placed my one free hand on his chest, over his heart. It was beating too fast. He was scared, indeed. But I was terrified—not only of what seemed like his almost certain short-term fate, but even more so for what this means for all of us.

We are all one.

And we are doing this to ourselves?

I intentionally slowed my breathing and made sure it was audible to him, hoping somehow it would be soothing. I began to chant "Ohm Shanti, Ohm Shanti, Ohm" over and over again in his ear. I had no idea what else to do.

I fixed my gaze upon his velvety eyes and attempted some sort of telepathic communication. "I see you, Bodhi."

And then right there,
my fingers as a pacifier,
and a hand on his heart,
face to face,
nose to nose,
eyes engaged,
I felt his heart
slow down,
and
stop.

I believe that if more of us had soulful encounters with animals, it would prompt us to change our behavior and our choices.

I know that it is just a matter of time. I have hope, and I have faith, that our hearts are designed to open, that they LONG for nothing more than to embrace ourselves, each other, and all beings.

Playing Chicken with Ram Dass

There was a guru who one morning gave each of his two disciples a chicken.

He told them, "Each of you, go now and take your chicken to a place where no one will see, kill it and return to me."

The men walked away into the forest.

After a brief time one of the disciples returned with a dead chicken and presented it to the guru. Day turned into night and then into day. The guru waited. Just around sunset, the second disciple returned carrying the chicken that he had been given.

It was very much alive.

The guru looked at him and said, "I told you to go to a place where no one will see and kill the chicken."

The man hung his head and replied, "Yes, Guruji. But everywhere I go, the chicken sees."

I have retired from the egotistical position of telling other people what they should or should not do.

However, I will put forth this unsolicited suggestion:

We are all animals (human and non-human). Please consider being kind to one another.

We are all one.
And we are doing
this to ourselves
and each other.

Ponder-ables:

Imagine yourself to be encircled by a ring of compassion. How far outside of yourself does this ring of compassion currently extend? Who/what is included and who/what is left out?

Can you relax and extend the diameter of this circle? Do you find this idea enticing or frightening? What might truly be at risk by doing so? What might truly be at risk by NOT doing so?

What would it mean for how we treat "others" if we were to realize that there's no such thing?

CHAPTER TWENTY-NINE:
ON FREEDOM & CONNECTION

"True freedom is always spiritual. It has something to do with your innermost being, which cannot be chained, handcuffed, or put into a jail."

—Rajneesh

May I make a confession? Please keep this on the down-low...

I don't care what my coaching clients say they want. I know what they truly want. Of course, this is simply my current belief and that does not mean it is true.

So, as with every word
put forth in this book,
ponder over yonder and
see
what
you
see.

At this moment, this is what I see...

Everything people consciously desire and intuitively long for is found within and through a foundation of *freedom and connection*. We are all born with these synergistic energy states inherent within us, and simply lose sight of and/or forget these attributes of our existence through the well-meaning (and short-term useful) processes of cultural conditioning and indoctrination.

We Are Born Into Connection

Babies are born into the energetic flow of Consciousness; and as such, are simultaneously free and connected to everything. More than that, really. It is not a connection in the strict sense of the word, but rather the TRUTH of our ONENESS, *which feels like connection.*

They are immersed in Oneness within the Ocean of Being, and progressively test out what it means to experience oneself as a wave, intimately part of the ocean yet cresting with self-expression.

Speaking of waves, we have all witnessed a baby literally "waving" her hand in front of her face, attempting to ascertain whether this particular appendage is part of her or separate from her, or both.

Certainly babies sense a connection to their parents or caregivers. I cannot remember much from my infancy, so please don't ask me how I am so certain. It sure does seem that way, though. And then, we (as babies) start the process of experiencing separation. This is in part our own doing via self-exploration, and partly what we are taught, primarily through example.

This is not to say that this process is bad. It has a well-intended purpose, mainly to assist you in "becoming somebody," developing some sense of self-reliance and know-how to get on within Relative Reality.

Although not bad, it is not entirely based in Truth. It has a high Utility Score, but a low Truth Score. It is *Useful* (to a point), but not (at a Foundational level) *Truthful*.

Can you imagine explaining to a toddler how this "little somebody" that they are becoming is nothing but a false self, and these apparent distinctions between him and his friends is just an illusion? Getting children to share toys is one thing and can be a fine elementary teaching lesson. Attempting to get buy-in from them on the concept that one cannot "own" anything as an illusory separate self would be painful on so many levels.

It seems there is a time and a place for progressive realizations to be fostered/ encouraged to emerge. Like the physical ocean, the Ocean of Being has a natural tide, an ebb and flow.

All will be revealed.

All in good time.

The Boomerang of Connection

Boomerangs are badass. If you don't agree, you are wrong; however, we can still be friends.

Imagine, if you would be so kind as to indulge me, that you have in your hands a boomerang. It represents your innate sense of connection and inherent Oneness with everything. This includes your connection to yourself, to apparent "others," and to the entirety of the world around you.

Boomerangs are designed to be thrown outwards and away from oneself, much like Oneness and connection are designed to be tested. Both are also inherently designed to return to the sender.

Side Note: There is evidence that other types of "non-returning" boomerangs have been used as deadly weapons in wars or hunting. Witness the recent discovery of an 800-year-old skeleton who apparently took a direct boomerang kill shot to his skull. This is not the type of boomerang of which I speak.

There are some tricks, and a learning curve, to successfully hurling a boomerang and having it come back to you. Likewise, there are some skill sets (and mindsets) when experimenting with Connection.

However, the most basic of all tenets would be:

STAY PUT AND PAY ATTENTION.

That is to say, after throwing your "rang" or questioning your connection to the rest of conscious creation, there is no more work to be done on your part. The boomerang, as well as your Connection to the Ocean of Being, is part of you, and therefore will make its way back to its origin.

It is literally
and figuratively
"out of your hands."

Yes, you could "do some work," chase after it, attempt to improve your position, maybe monitor the path of the boomerang in order to feel more secure that it will be returning, or just worry about it (because that's always helpful). The most popular "work" tends to be racing after the boomerang on its initial outward path, AKA "seeking." Of course, this is a fruitless endeavor, as it's already made the turn and is looking to come back, only to find Home Base is empty with you many steps behind.

Live Free or Die

The above declaration is the state motto of New Hampshire, circa 1945. I like it, except that it is structured as an either/or, when in truth it is a both/and.

We are all
born free
and
we will all
kick the
oxygen habit
eventually.

There are many types of freedoms, including:

- Freedom of belief
- Freedom of speech
- Freedom of the press
- Freedom of association
- Freedom of religion
- Freedom from bondage (exemptions include consenting adults with a safe word)

The above freedoms and many more like them are all well and good. Personally, I would much rather have them than not. That being said, these are not the types of freedoms that I am pointing towards in this essay.

Authentic Freedom

There is a meta-level freedom that trumps all other freedoms, without which none of these important but secondary freedoms mean a damn thing.

We can call it *Authentic Freedom*. It is THE Freedom into which you are born. It cannot be given to you by a higher authority or passed into law through legislation. It would be silly to go to war in order to attain it or protect it, as it is already and always within you.

Authentic Freedom is freedom from fear.
Authentic Freedom is freedom from self-improvement.
Authentic Freedom is freedom from supposed imperfection.
Authentic Freedom is freedom from seeking.
Authentic Freedom is freedom from the illusion of separation.

Authentic Freedom can only be (figuratively) imprisoned by the innocent mis-use of the power of our minds. This prison is invisible and 100% of our own creation.

What is the first and most crucial step to escaping from a prison?

Recognizing
that you're
in a prison!

And in this case, thankfully, this is the one and only necessary step. Simple recognition that the door is wide open, and then allowing whatever action (or non-action) makes the most sense based on this insight. (That damn Heisenberg Principle again.)

"Why do you stay in prison when the door is so wide open? Move outside the tangle of fear-thinking. The entrance door to the sanctuary is inside you."—Rumi

Give the People What They Want

I made a confession and a bold claim: I know what people truly want, at a meta-level— the recognition and embodiment of their inherent freedom and connection.

To keep with the bold claims, I also suggested that each of us already possesses these attributes from birth, and they cannot be taken from us, or given to us by others.

If it is true that we all are born free and that we are all One, how is it we feel otherwise so much of the time? And what are we supposed to do in order to feel what is right there below the surface, at the core of our being?

It is simple and yet perplexing to our conditioned mind. We have forgotten who and what we are. We have forgotten we are part of the Divine.

We have forgotten
that we are God.

The basic tenets of boomeranging apply
to most endeavors, especially the spiritual
journey:

STAY PUT AND PAY ATTENTION.

Ponder-ables:

Do you currently have any desires that are
not inherently grounded in connection and
freedom?

How do you throw away your innate sense
of connection, and then seek it outside of
yourself?

Would you consider staying put and paying
attention?

Can you sense your imaginary prison?

Are you willing to walk through the open
cell door to freedom?

Have you forgotten? Welcome Back.

DO NOTHING

CHAPTER THIRTY:
SILENCE & ORIGINAL GRACE

Diligent study and dedicated practice will only take you so far. At some point, you've gotta say FUCK IT, and step off the ledge. And when it feels like you're falling... dive.

Know Thyself in Silence

"Jesus Christ knew he was God. So, wake up and find out eventually who you really are. In our culture, of course, they'll say you're crazy and you're blasphemous, and they'll either put you in jail or in a nut house (which is pretty much the same thing). However, if you wake up in India and tell your friends and relations, 'My goodness, I've just discovered that I'm God,' they'll laugh and say, 'Oh, congratulations, at last you found out.'"

—Allan Watts

It certainly isn't my place to tell you that you're God, or proclaim that I am as well, or that your besties and your worsties, and even, or perhaps especially, that the vilest characters you condemn on the news are all, as Ram Dass liked to say, "just God in drag."

Who the hell am I to make such an assertion?

The most I'll do, I suppose,
is to put forth a gentle suggestion
that you get still and silent,
look within, and see what you see.

That's about the extent of what feels worthwhile to share in this final essay. (It is an essay about silence and grace, after all.) It is a bit crazy because I love words, and I love pondering and pontificating upon these topics. Writing and speaking are the only semi-creative or modestly artistic skills I possess. I can't draw, paint, or play a musical instrument to save my life.

Sadly though, words will always fail me when the topic is Truth. Words are just symbols, an attempt (always in vain) to convey the formless in the form of language. Except for poets. That subset of talented wordsmiths is way beyond me. To be able to use minimal language, to make it sing, so others can hear the music behind the words... I am in awe of spiritual poets such as Rumi. Instead of their seemingly surgical precision and minimal word choice, I'm prone to vocabulary vomit.

Perhaps that is why this new-found sense of silence is not concerning to me, but rather quite a relief.

This reminds me of a parable addressing the trifecta of silence, grace and jumping off ledges.

There was an ancient kingdom separated from the outside world by a tremendous wall over 100 feet high. The citizens of the kingdom believed that on the other side of this wall was God, or The Gods, and Truth. After a particularly harsh winter, with their faith being challenged and running low on food, a contingent of them decided to see what was outside of the wall, and what wisdom it might have to share. They banded together and created a human pyramid, with the final person just barely able to grab the top of the wall and climb onto the ledge. He stood atop the wall and looked down at the other side... and jumped.

The kingdom folks were baffled and upset. They had lost one of their own and were none the wiser as to what was on the other side of the wall. So, round two, same plan, but they made the final guy PROMISE not to jump, to climb back down and inform the community of what he had seen. However, upon reaching the top and looking over, like his predecessor, he took a swan dive over to the other side.

Round Three. This was getting out of hand. They decided to have the King's daughter be the last one to ascend to the top. Surely, she wouldn't jump. But as an extra measure, they tied a rope around her waist. As she reached the top, she looked over the wall, and of course she jumped. But they were able to pull her back up and bring her to the village center for a full debriefing. Upon asking her to explain what she had seen and why she had also jumped, they realized that although she was beaming with joy, she had gone totally mute.

The more I snuggle up with and get a sense of Truth, the more I realize how silly it sounds when I try to talk or write about it. The closer I seem to get, the more I sound like those generic "good vibes only" memes dominating social media these days. Does the fact that it's a popular meme and 69% of all sorority members have it tattooed above their ass crack make it any less true?

I don't think so. But I'm also drawn to silence because nothing feels truer than silence.

The Source of Original Grace

To round out this essay and the written portion of this book, I would like to share a short story on Original Grace, and a suggestion for a question:

Once upon a time there was a five-year-old girl who had recently been blessed with a baby brother. She was over the moon for this little boy. The parents were thrilled with her enthusiasm and outpouring of love and attention towards him. However, she kept asking if she could have some time alone with the baby. Although they had no evidence to suspect any malicious intent, they'd heard of older kids sometimes becoming jealous of younger siblings for stealing the attention of the parents. So, they agreed, but had a Nanny Cam in the nursery so they could monitor what transpired.

Here is what they witnessed:

The daughter tiptoed into the nursery and up to the crib. Sticking her face through the wooden slats, she whispered "Baby brother, wake up. Can you remind me what God is like? I'm starting to forget."

And that's what has happened to all of us— we've just forgotten, become distracted, lost our bearings. It's not a reflection of our unworthiness, but rather just that we're human. The beautiful thing is we are always just one moment, one thought away from remembering who and what we are, and returning, blissfully, to our birthplace, a state of original grace.

Upgrade Your Questions and Tolerance for Grace

Although it may be true that there are no stupid questions, it does seem as though some are better than others, or at least more fruitful. I've upgraded my questions over the years, from "What's wrong with me (or them)?" to "What do I truly want?" to "What tends to pull me out of oneness and into the illusion of separation?" The volume of questions continues to shrink, as does the apparent complexity of the answers.

I've recently landed on just one: "How much Grace can I tolerate?"

My answer is variable day to day and even moment to moment. However, the foundational presupposition of this inquiry is why the juice is disproportionately ginormous compared to the squeeze.

And that is this: God is lurking around every corner, waiting to pounce and overwhelm us with the Grace and Love that is both our birthright and our True Nature. However, being compassionate and patient, God will wait until we are adequately able to accept such a gift and the accompanying insights. Therefore, instead of building up your resilience or GRIT or whatever the latest self-help hashtag of the day may be, or attempting to *do something* in order to feel worthy, may I suggest you simply ask yourself:

How much Grace can I tolerate?

And then
open your heart
and whisper
"Bring it on."

Ponder-ables

What if silence wasn't silent?

What if there was always a beautiful melody in the background?

How might you effortlessly remember your original grace?

How much grace can you tolerate?

CONCLUSION

So, we arrive at the end.

The end of this book; and perhaps,
if our tolerance for Grace is sufficient,
at least the beginning of the end
of our seeking (and our suffering).

Thank you for allowing me the privilege of
joining you in this ongoing exploration.

We've pondered together upon many diverse
subjects, including, but not limited to:

Teddy Bears
Feces (lots of feces)
Worry
Forgiveness
Bumper Stickers
Love
Teamwork
Fetishes (lots of fetishes)
Letting Go
Ego
Naked Yoga
Meditation
Non-Duality
Fight Club
Freedom & Connection
Silence & Grace

This exploration is not intended to be the final word on any of these subjects, but more of a jumping-off point.

As you continue to ponder and explore for yourself, remember to relax; there is nothing you need to do and there is nowhere to go. You are already doing it (life) and you are always home (abiding in the eternal presence).

You will likely be drawn to look outside of yourself for knowledge from time to time...

Not to worry, it's all good.

Keep in mind, however, that Wisdom is always and only found within.

And the gateway within is the question: "Who Am I?"

If you will indulge me one final parable:

A young Indian religious student takes on the meditative inquiry, "Who am I?" When she asks for guidance, she is told to ascend the mountain and ask one of the Swami gurus residing in the caves. She climbs for many hours and reaches a cave, goes inside, and asks the Swami, "Can you tell me, Who am I?" The Swami replies that such a question is too big for him, and she should seek out such knowledge from a Swami further up the mountain.

She climbs for several more hours and arrives at another cave and asks the resident Swami the same question: "Who Am I?" He replies much the same, that she must ask someone more awakened, higher still up the mountain.

So, she climbs through the night and arrives at a cave on the peak of the mountain. Exhausted, she enters and asks the Swami, "Who am I?" The Swami looks up from her meditation and replies, "Who's asking?"

And finally, the best news of all (drum roll optional):

Let there be no doubt...

This
Is
The
Fun
Part

This entire human incarnation, this life, your life.

Within this level of consciousness, this is the best damn game in town.

In all its glory,
even when it gets gory,
all of it, the bitter and the sweet;

squeeze it fully and savor every last drop.

Say it with me,
This is the fun part...
This is the fun part.

APPEΠDİX

MetaGnosis Audio Sessions

Note: MetaGnosis Sessions are available via the QR code or link at the end of this introduction.

There are many modes of transportation on the Spiritual Exploration Highway. Throughout this book we have been pondering upon a multitude of topics, and I have done my best to suggest a gentle relaxation of our intellectual faculties on this endeavor; to instead drop into the space of the felt sense of the body and an opening of the heart.

Easier suggested than done, no doubt. The pull of the intellect is strong and sufficiently ingrained, indeed.

To that end, let's switch up the input source, and introduce some exploration from the auditory/somatic side of the equation.

These audio sessions could be considered a hybrid of guided meditation and hypnosis. Each one is briefly described below:

The Do-Nothing Meditation

The (in)famous Do Nothing Meditation has a long history in the Buddhist tradition as well as with many more recent teachers, including mine, Adyashanti. There are two parts to this session: the first is a short explanation on how to do nothing (trickier than one might think), and a second part where you are invited to do nothing for a ten-minute meditation.

Compassionate Curiosity

In this meditative inquiry session, we will be evoking and abiding in the energetic emotional states of compassion and curiosity.

Curiosity is the engine that drives our journey within eschatological realism, our ever-evolving trajectory towards spiritual maturity and realization of our True Self.

Compassion is the fuel of the heart.

I suggest you choose one specific issue or problem you are dealing with currently. It could be an ongoing emotion, a habit or simply a personality trait. Choose something you've been trying to stop or get rid of for some time now.

Instead of attempting to exorcize yourself of said trait, habit, or emotion, you will "invite it in for tea." This "bad" element will be welcomed into your heart and enveloped with deep compassion and a fierce curiosity.

Plant Prophets

This session is a bit different.

I would like to share with you the wisdom that has been so graciously gifted to me by the plants.

So, sit back
Relax
And hang on...

Access MetaGnosis Session Page:

Link: **https://RenegadeLifeCoach.com/ metagnosis-audio-sessions**

Note: Personalized MetaGnosis sessions are available from Hypnotherapist Coach Bill Gladwell - hypnosisforhumans.com

RESOURCES FOR FURTHER EXPLORATION

I invite you to continue your exploration of The Three Principles and Non-Duality with some resources from my favorite coaches, teachers, and authors below:

The Three Principles

Sydney Banks

Books: *The Missing Link, The Enlightened Gardner*

Website: sydbanks.com

Michael Neill

Books: *Supercoach, The Inside-Out Revolution, The Space Within*

Website: michealneill.org

Jamie Smart

Books: *Clarity, Results*

Website: https://www.jamiesmart.com

George & Linda Pransky

Books: *The Relationship Handbook*

Website: pranskyandassociates.com

Amy Johnson

Books: *The Little Book of Big Change, Just a Thought*

Website: dramyjohnson.com

Ken Manning, Robin Charbit, Sandra Krot (business)

Books: *Invisible Power*

Website: insightprinciples.com

Garret Kramer (sports)

Books: *The Path of No Resistance, Stillpower*

Website: garretkramer.com

Non-Duality

Adyashanti

Books: *The Way of Liberation, The Impact of Awakening, The End of Your World*

Website: adyashanti.opengatesangha.org

Garret Kramer

Books: *True Self: Notes on the Essence of Being*

Website: garretkramer.com

Jeff Foster

Books: *The Deepest Acceptance, You Were Never Broken, The Joy of True Meditation*

Website: lifewithoutacentre.com

Rupert Spira

Books: *The Nature of Consciousness, Being Aware of Being Aware*

Website: rupertspira.com

ACKNOWLEDGMENTS

I am one lucky bastard.

The amount of guidance, acceptance, and unconditional love of which I have been the recipient throughout my life is staggering and wholly undeserved.

I would like to highlight a few individuals who have supported me in general and specifically on this project, and offer up my heartfelt gratitude.

To Rich and Dianne, my esteemed parental units: although they claim I was an easy kid, it couldn't have always been easy to understand me. That made no difference to them; they just loved me and encouraged me to do what made me happy. And here we are...

To Michelle, my wife, co-pilot, and best friend: The variety and depth of support you've bestowed upon me is immeasurable, from your fierce loyalty to the cheerleading that I occasionally need, to the CTFD-ing I also occasionally need, to the tech support (like turning on the computer), which I *always* need, to the seemingly effortless outpouring of your unconditional love. My mother is right: you are an angel.

To Dave, my brother from another mother and fellow journeyman: I sense that our paths have been parallel for lifetimes, I'm grateful they crossed in this one. Love you, man.

To Brother Bradley, The Apostle: the contemplative urban hikes, your encouragement to speak my voice and do my work my way, your eager willingness to read the very rough draft of this manuscript (no easy task), and your friendship are treasured gifts, thank you.

To Dylan and Torrie, my other-side-travel guides. Without your friendship and expertise, Plant Prophets would never have been birthed.

To Bill Gladwell, your hypnosis mentorship and perfectionistic production of the audio sessions was the cherry on top of this banana split of a project. Yum!

To all my coaching clients, thank you for allowing me the privilege of exploring with you. I have gained more insights from witnessing your courageous willingness to dive deep than I could ever reciprocate.

To all the coaches and teachers who have influenced my understanding and continue to prompt further insights, including Jamie Smart, Michael Neill, Amy Johnson, Garrett

Kramer, George and Linda Pransky, and Adyashanti.

To Rob Bell, you gave me the permission (that I thought I needed) to intentionally leave my energetic imprint on that which I create; to ask, "What needs to be expressed in this moment through me?" and to ignore "best practices"; to structure sentences as I wish them to be read; to create for the sheer enjoyment of the process; and to fuck curating for any particular target audience, and instead set the dinner table with my best cuisine and see who sniffs it out and shows up.

To John Mabry, Janeen Jones, and the good folks at Apocryphile Press, thank you for supporting authors with something slightly atypical to share, and putting up with my "charming idiosyncrasies."

And finally, to God herself AKA Source, Spirit, Universal Energy, Awareness, Buddha Nature, The Infinite, Love, Dog: thank you for your undying persistence; you kept knocking on the door, occasionally pounding on it to wake me up. I heard you. I see you now.

ABOUT THE AUTHOR

Stephen Ladd (preferred pronouns Us/ We/One) is a coach, author, podcaster, and speaker specializing in existential constipation – the sense of being stuck, jammed up or blocked within the bowels of everyday life or on the spiritual journey (which are the same thing, of course).

Stephen traversed an unorthodox path of education and training, combining traditional academics, mentorships, and off-the-grid journeys. His formal studies were focused on Psychology, Philosophy and Comparative Religion.

Stephen's coaching is grounded in compassionate curiosity, connection and mutual exploration into how human animals experience the external world, the depth of our True Nature, and the authentic freedom that is available as our minds settle and allow space for our Innate Wisdom to blossom within us.

Contact Stephen for inquiries regarding coaching, speaking, or meeting up over some good bourbon:

Website: RenegadeLifeCoach.com
Email: Coach@RenegadeLifeCoach.com
Instagram: @renegadelifecoach

Made in USA - North Chelmsford, MA
1314489_9781955821872
05.16.2022 0823